S. Hrg. 113–636

KEEPING UP WITH A CHANGING ECONOMY: INDEXING THE MINIMUM WAGE

HEARING

OF THE

COMMITTEE ON HEALTH, EDUCATION, LABOR, AND PENSIONS

UNITED STATES SENATE

ONE HUNDRED THIRTEENTH CONGRESS

FIRST SESSION

ON

EXAMINING KEEPING UP WITH A CHANGING ECONOMY, FOCUSING ON INDEXING THE MINIMUM WAGE

MARCH 14, 2013

Printed for the use of the Committee on Health, Education, Labor, and Pensions

Available via the World Wide Web: http://www.gpo.gov/fdsys/

U.S. GOVERNMENT PUBLISHING OFFICE

94–431 PDF   WASHINGTON : 2015

For sale by the Superintendent of Documents, U.S. Government Publishing Office
Internet: bookstore.gpo.gov   Phone: toll free (866) 512–1800; DC area (202) 512–1800
Fax: (202) 512–2104   Mail: Stop IDCC, Washington, DC 20402–0001

COMMITTEE ON HEALTH, EDUCATION, LABOR, AND PENSIONS

TOM HARKIN, Iowa, *Chairman*

BARBARA A. MIKULSKI, Maryland
PATTY MURRAY, Washington
BERNARD SANDERS (I), Vermont
ROBERT P. CASEY, JR., Pennsylvania
KAY R. HAGAN, North Carolina
AL FRANKEN, Minnesota
MICHAEL F. BENNET, Colorado
SHELDON WHITEHOUSE, Rhode Island
TAMMY BALDWIN, Wisconsin
CHRISTOPHER S. MURPHY, Connecticut
ELIZABETH WARREN, Massachusetts

LAMAR ALEXANDER, Tennessee
MICHAEL B. ENZI, Wyoming
RICHARD BURR, North Carolina
JOHNNY ISAKSON, Georgia
RAND PAUL, Kentucky
ORRIN G. HATCH, Utah
PAT ROBERTS, Kansas
LISA MURKOWSKI, Alaska
MARK KIRK, Illlinois
TIM SCOTT, South Carolina

PAMELA J. SMITH, *Staff Director, Chief Counsel*
LAUREN McFERRAN, *Deputy Staff Director*
DAVID P. CLEARY, *Republican Staff Director*

(II)

CONTENTS

STATEMENTS

THURSDAY, MARCH 14, 2013

(III)

KEEPING UP WITH A CHANGING ECONOMY: INDEXING THE MINIMUM WAGE

THURSDAY, MARCH 14, 2013

U.S. SENATE,
COMMITTEE ON HEALTH, EDUCATION, LABOR, AND PENSIONS,
Washington, DC.

The committee met, pursuant to notice, at 10:05 a.m. in room SD–430, Dirksen Senate Office Building, Hon. Tom Harkin, chairman of the committee, presiding.

Present: Senators Harkin, Alexander, and Warren.

OPENING STATEMENT OF SENATOR HARKIN

The CHAIRMAN. Good morning. The Senate Health, Education, Labor, and Pensions Committee will please come to order.

For several years now, I have held hearings in this committee focusing on the need to bolster the middle class in this country and to help restore the American Dream. The American Dream is supposed to be about building a better life through work. If you work hard and play by the rules, you should be able to support your family, raise your kids, get them a good education, enjoy some of the accoutrements of life: housing, clothing, a decent vacation once in a while, and retirement.

But today, tens of millions of hardworking Americans, who are earning at or near the minimum wage, can't even aspire to live a middle-class life or achieve the American Dream. They are falling further and further behind. We need to do more to support these workers as they try to build opportunity for their families and their futures. A critical first step is to ensure that they earn a fair day's pay for a hard day's work. That is why last week I joined with Congressman George Miller to introduce the Fair Minimum Wage Act of 2013, to provide a long-overdue increase in the Federal minimum wage.

The bill would gradually increase the minimum wage to $10.10 an hour in three annual steps, and then link future increases to the cost of living, so that people who are trying to get ahead don't fall behind as the economy grows.

Today's hearing will focus, I hope the most, on indexing the minimum wage. This is the first hearing in this committee to look at indexing the minimum wage in more than 20 years.

Over the past four decades, Congress has raised the minimum wage five times, but these raises have come sporadically and after long stretches with no raise. The subsequent increases have not brought the wage up to its past level, and so the real value of the minimum wage has declined significantly.

The minimum wage right now is, in fact, worth 31 percent less than at its peak in 1968, even as productivity has soared. That is what that chart shows. It shows productivity going up. Interestingly enough, real average wages right now are about where they were in 1970; real average wages. But the real minimum wage, as you can see, has gone down about 31 percent; real, when you take inflation into account.

If the minimum wage had kept pace with inflation since 1968, today it would be $10.56 an hour, and a full-time worker would earn about $22,000 a year under the minimum wage. Instead, now it is $7.25 and the earnings are about $15,000 a year. Actually, that is a poverty wage.

I pointed out the other day, also, that in the 1970s, the minimum wage was about 20 percent higher than the poverty level. Today, it is 20 percent less than the poverty level.

This has hurt, seriously hurt, the standard of living for low-wage workers and their families. As a result, more and more low-wage families are forced to rely on safety net programs like food stamps, and housing assistance, and things like that to ensure that they can survive. And when millions are barely surviving because of low wages, they just cannot hope to join the middle class, and everyone gets hurt, especially our economy.

The middle class is the backbone of our economy, and we have to grow that middle class to have a growing economy, I believe, in the long run. Businesses need customers to buy things if they want to grow and prosper. But when workers earn a poverty wage, they do not have purchasing power, they cannot help the economy thrive.

That is why so many businesses, large and small, from the CEO of Costco to the record store owner that we will hear from here today, they support a higher minimum wage, and support indexing it so that it will no longer lose value in the future.

I think we stand at a rare moment of opportunity where we can do what is right for the economy, and at the same time, do what is simply right. A fair minimum wage that is predictable, with modest increases that keep wages steadily growing in pace with inflation, rather than falling behind, I think, will benefit everyone. Indexing will do all of these things. That is why 10 States have already implemented indexing, and we will hear from one of them today. At the Federal level, this policy is long overdue.

I have this chart that shows the 10 States that already do index, and as you can see, it ranges from very progressive liberal States like Vermont, to conservative States like Florida, and Missouri, and Arizona, and Montana. So it does not favor one area of the country over the other, it is kind of spread around, but 10 States that, I think, represent various places on the political spectrum; various parts of the political spectrum have already decided to index their minimum wage.

Of course, it must be done right. We have to be sure to set an adequate minimum wage in the first place, before we index it because obviously, if you set it too low, then you index it, you are always going to be way behind. That is why my legislation would first increase the minimum wage to $10.10 an hour, over 3 years, and then index it after that.

Once we make sure that the minimum wage is an adequate wage, indexing means that American workers will be able to count on fair wages in the future. No longer will low-wage workers go years without even a penny raise.

This chart shows since 2009—since the last minimum wage was fully implemented—what has happened to the costs of electricity, rent, food, childcare, and mass transit—they have all gone up 4 percent to 12.5 percent. People who are at the minimum wage and stuck at that, are falling further and further behind because they are spending most of their earned income on these items: housing, childcare, food, auto repair, rent, electricity. That is why I think indexing is going to be so important to put in place.

I want to thank our witnesses for being here today. I look forward to an informative discussion.

[The prepared statement of Senator Harkin follows:]

Prepared Statement of Senator Harkin

For several years now I have held hearings focusing on the need to bolster the middle class in this country and restore the American Dream. The American Dream is supposed to be about building a better life. If you work hard and play by the rules, you should be able to support your family, join the middle class, and build a brighter future for your children.

But today, tens of millions of hardworking Americans who are earning at or near the minimum wage can't even *aspire* to live a middle-class life or achieve the American Dream. Instead, they are falling further and further behind. We need to do more to support these workers as they try to build opportunity for their families and their futures. A critical first step is to ensure that they earn a fair day's pay for a hard day's work. That is why last week I joined with Congressman George Miller to introduce the Fair Minimum Wage Act of 2013, which would provide a long-overdue increase in the Federal minimum wage.

This bill will gradually increase the minimum wage to $10.10 an hour in three annual steps, and then link future increases in the minimum wage to the cost of living, so that people who are trying to get ahead don't fall behind as our economy grows.

Today's hearing will focus specifically on indexing the minimum wage. This is the first hearing in this committee to look at indexing the minimum wage in more than 20 years.

Over the past four decades, Congress has raised the minimum wage five times. But these raises have come sporadically and after long stretches with no raise. The subsequent increases have not brought the wage up to its past levels, and so the real value of the wage has declined significantly. The minimum wage in fact is worth 31 percent less than at its peak in 1968, even as productivity has soared.

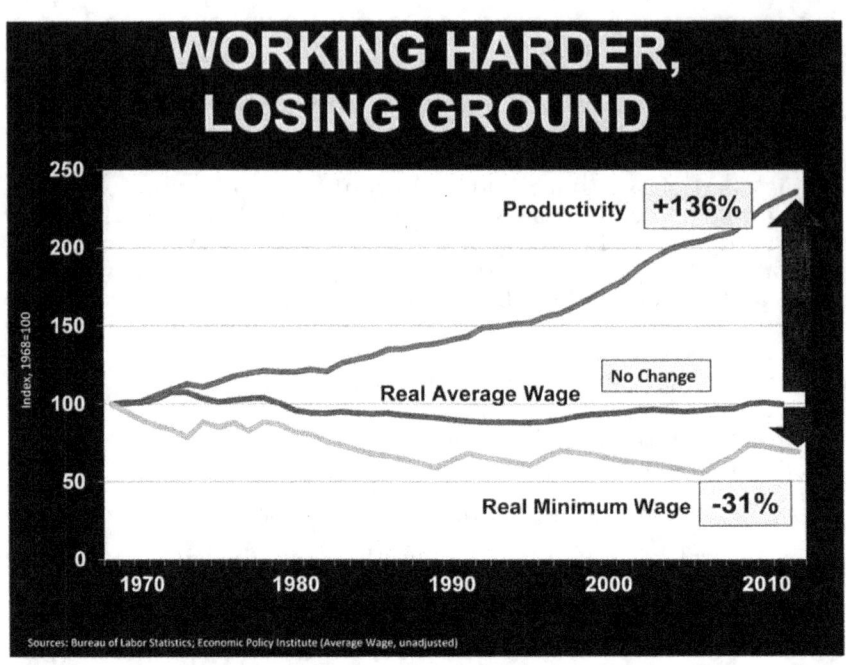

WORKING HARDER, LOSING GROUND

Productivity +136%

Real Average Wage — No Change

Real Minimum Wage -31%

Sources: Bureau of Labor Statistics; Economic Policy Institute (Average Wage, unadjusted)

This means that as the economy has grown and corporate profits are at an all-time high, tens of millions of low-wage workers and their families have almost a third less buying power than 45 years ago. If the minimum wage had kept pace with inflation since 1968, today it would be $10.56 and a full-time worker would earn nearly $22,000. Instead, the minimum wage is $7.25 and a full-time worker earns only $15,000 a year. It is a poverty wage.

This has seriously hurt the standard of living for low-wage workers and their families. As a result, many low-wage families are forced to rely on safety net programs like food stamps and housing assistance to ensure that they can survive. And when millions of workers are barely surviving because of low wages, they cannot hope to join the middle class. This ends up hurting everyone, especially our economy.

It's important to make clear who is earning at or near the minimum wage. My bill would provide raises to 30 million workers— 21 million workers who earn below $10.10 and 9 million who earn just over $10.10. The Economic Policy Institute has run the numbers to help us paint a picture of who these 30 million workers are, and they are not who we might expect. For instance, they are not all teenagers. In fact, 88 percent of people who would get a raise are adults age 20 or over, not teenagers. We also know that the majority, 56 percent, are women and nearly half, 46 percent, are people of color.

And these are not all part-time workers, either. Most of the workers, 55 percent, are full-time workers, and almost all, 86 percent, work at least 20 hours a week. Workers who will get a raise under my bill are not uneducated, either: 44 percent have some college or more education.

Finally, these are not workers in rich families just supplementing the higher earnings of other family members. Fifty-five percent of the workers have family income of $40,000 or less and 62 percent have family income under $50,000. These workers rely on their earnings to survive: the workers who will get a raise under my bill earn half of their family's income, on average; if the workers are parents, they earn 59 percent of their family's income.

The middle class is the backbone of our economy, and we must grow our middle class in order to have a growing economy in the long run. Businesses need customers to buy things if they want to grow and prosper. But when workers earn a poverty wage and have no purchasing power, they can't help the economy thrive. That's one reason why so many businesses large and small—from the CEO of Costco to the record store owner we will hear from today—support a higher minimum wage, and support indexing the minimum wage to inflation so that it will no longer lose value.

We stand at a rare moment of opportunity—where we can do what is right for the economy, and at the same time, do what is simply *right*. A fair minimum wage that is predictable, with modest increases that keep wages steadily growing in pace with inflation, rather than falling behind, benefits everyone. Indexing will do all of these things. That is why 10 States have already implemented this policy, and we will hear from one of them today.

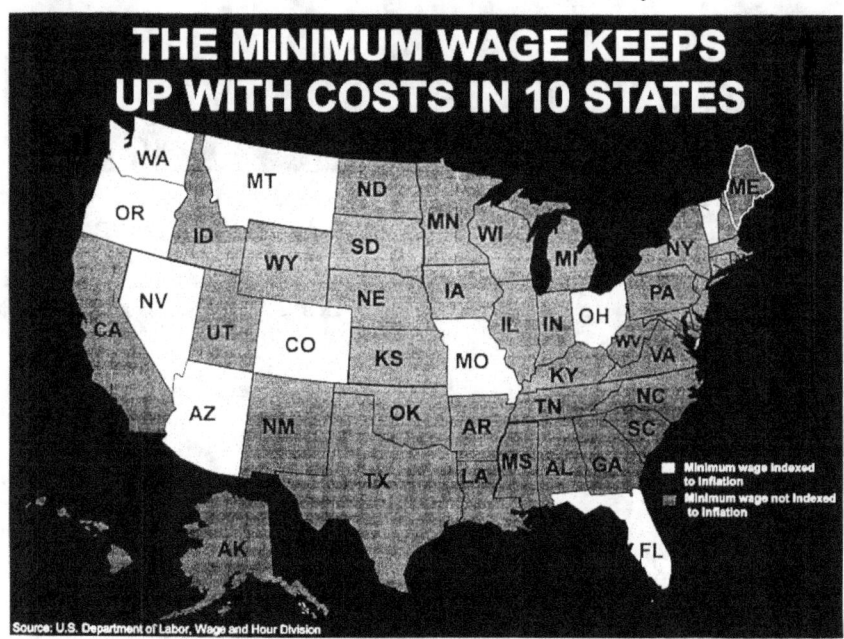

At the Federal level, this policy is long overdue.

Of course, indexing the minimum wage must be done right. We have to be sure to set an adequate minimum wage in the first place, before locking it in in real terms for the indefinite future. That is why my legislation would first increase the minimum wage to $10.10 an hour, phased in through three increases spread out over 3 years.

Once we make sure that the minimum wage is an adequate wage, indexing means that American workers will be able to count on fair wages in the future. No longer will low-wage workers go years without even a penny raise.

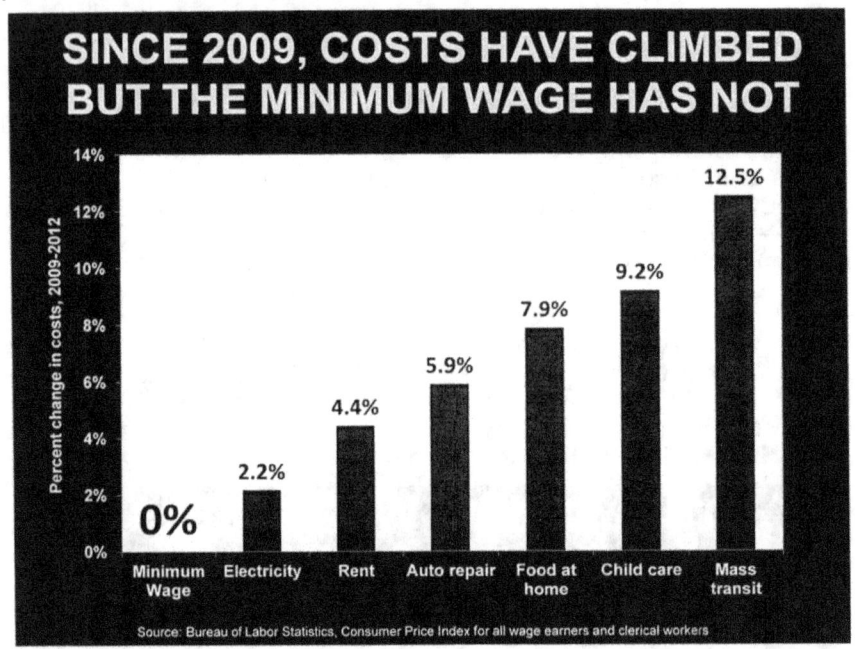

SINCE 2009, COSTS HAVE CLIMBED BUT THE MINIMUM WAGE HAS NOT

Source: Bureau of Labor Statistics, Consumer Price Index for all wage earners and clerical workers

When groceries get more expensive or the gas or electric bills go up, when the bus fare climbs again or the rent goes up—these workers, who typically must live paycheck-to-paycheck, will have the assurance that they have a raise coming to them. Indexing the minimum wage, then, not only helps working families keep up with the economy and deal with rising costs, it also gives them peace of mind.

I want to thank our witnesses for being here today, and I look forward to an informative discussion of this critically important issue.

And now, I will turn to Senator Alexander for opening comments.

OPENING STATEMENT OF SENATOR ALEXANDER

Senator ALEXANDER. Thanks, Mr. Chairman.

Thanks for the hearing, and thanks to each of the witnesses for making the time to come here.

I am afraid the Chairman and I have a difference of opinion here. This is a very well-intentioned idea, but I am afraid it will have the effect of hurting the very people we are trying to help, and hurting the people who are the employees, and hurting the people who are in the best position to help, and that would be the employers.

Let me explain why I say that. Let's take a couple of examples of individuals whom I will call Paul and Jennifer.

Paul lives in a rural part of Tennessee. He is 16 years old, still lives at home. He wants his first job. He wants to make a little money for college or a car, because he doesn't have the cash. Why am I talking about a teenager? Because the typical, or half, of minimum wage workers are actually a young person aged 16 to 24. Eighty percent of those youths are working part-time. Sixty-two percent of them are enrolled in school, and their average income is three times the poverty guideline for a family of four.

Now, will raising the minimum wage help this young man find a job or will it eliminate the job he wants to help earn some extra money? Will it saw off the first rung of the economic ladder of success, which will help him climb up that ladder, and earn something that would be more like a maximum wage instead of a minimum wage?

Or let's take Jennifer, who is 29, who lives in Nashville. She is a songwriter. She might be working, as most songwriters in Nashville are, at an extra job earning some extra money. She would represent the other half of the minimum wage workers: female, unmarried, working part-time. Three out of four have household incomes above the poverty guideline. Only 4 percent are single parents working full-time.

The problem is that in each case, the job which Paul and Jennifer might get might be eliminated by the increased costs on employers. We have witnesses here today who will talk about that, but let me give an example.

I recently met with a franchise group that owns 20 fast food restaurants in the DC area. They employ 542 people. Hospitality and restaurant companies are the largest employers of low-income, minority, largely young people. Now here is how they make a profit.

First they pay their Social Security and Medicare taxes for each employee. Then they have a menu labeling mandate they pay, we require that; that's $1,000 per restaurant. Then local government has some sick leave mandates; that goes on top of their costs. And next year, here comes the health care law with a more expensive health care plan or a $2,000 per employee penalty. The $2,000 would add up to $1 million in new costs for them. If they decide to offer new insurance, it could be even more expensive. Those are the expenses they have before we would come in with a new 39 percent increase in the cost of labor.

So I will be listening to the testimony today to try to hear whether this well-intentioned idea will hurt the people it is trying to help, or will help the people it is trying to help.

Just to conclude, Mr. Chairman, Christina Romer, who was President Obama's Council of Economic Advisers Chair said in *The New York Times* last week that, ''Raising the minimum wage can displace poor workers with more affluent ones who have higher skills.''

And economist David Neumark at the University of California and William Wascher surveyed more than 100 major academic studies on the impact of the minimum wage and determined that 85 percent of them found a negative employment effect on low-skilled workers.

I am afraid one reason we still have 12 million unemployed Americans is we have increasingly made it more expensive to hire full-time employees, and this would add to that cost.

Thank you, Mr. Chairman.

The CHAIRMAN. Thank you, Senator Alexander.

We have one panel. I will go through and introduce the panel, and then we will commence our comments.

First is Mr. Brad Avakian. Did I get it right? Avakian. Has been Commissioner of the Oregon Bureau of Labor and Industries since 2008. He oversees implementation of Oregon's voter-enacted minimum wage, which is indexed to inflation. Commissioner Avakian has served in both the Oregon State Senate and Oregon House of Representatives, and previously he was a civil rights attorney. He is a graduate of Oregon State University and Lewis & Clark Law School.

I will yield to our distinguished Senator from Massachusetts for purposes of introducing our next witness.

Senator WARREN. Our witness is Dr. Arin Dube. Welcome, Dr. Dube. We are glad to have you here. He is a specialist on the economic impact of minimum wage. He is an Assistant Professor of Economics at UMASS Amherst. Mr. Chairman, I have to tell you, Amherst is a place where only the ''H'' is silent. That is what we like to say in Massachusetts. Welcome.

He has his B.S. from Stanford, his Ph.D. from the University of Chicago. His post-doctoral work was at University of California at Berkeley.

Welcome, Dr. Dube.

The CHAIRMAN. Thank you very much, Senator. Welcome, Dr. Dube.

Next we have Mr. Lew Prince, the managing partner and CEO of Vintage Vinyl in St. Louis, MO. In 1979, Mr. Prince and his business partner, Tom Ray, started with 300 records at the local farmer's market. Today Vintage Vinyl is the largest independent music store in the Midwest, and one of the largest in the country.

Interestingly enough, I was having lunch last Friday with a friend of mine, just having lunch, right. And he said to me, ''When was the last time you were in a record store?'' I thought, you know, I used to love to go to record stores. Look through the vinyl, and then you started getting compact discs. You could go, and you could see, and it was a just a pleasure. I had to stop and think. There aren't any more.

Mr. PRINCE. Oh, you'd love mine.

The CHAIRMAN. I think I would love yours.

[Laughter.]

Mr. PRINCE. Seven thousand square feet of music love.

[Laughter.]

The CHAIRMAN. I'd spend the whole day there. Anyway, it was just interesting that it was even the topic of our conversation, but it came up, and we were lamenting the fact that we do not have record stores anymore.

That then led into a discussion on Internet piracy. And my friend said to me,

''Isn't it an interesting thing, that if you walked into a record store, and took a CD, and walked out without paying for it, you would get arrested for thievery. But if you download it free, you get away with it.''

Well, anyway, I did not mean to get into that.

Mr. PRINCE. The technology is there to protect copyrights.

The CHAIRMAN. Yes.

Mr. PRINCE. I would love to talk to you about that.

The CHAIRMAN. It is just interesting.

Mr. PRINCE. I know a lot about it. I have a company that is designed to protect copyrights on the Internet.

The CHAIRMAN. Well, because it was happenstance that we happened to——

Senator ALEXANDER. I would like to talk with you. We have a big problem with that in Nashville.

The CHAIRMAN. Well, that is right. You've got an interest in that.

Senator ALEXANDER. We might have another hearing.

[Laughter.]

The CHAIRMAN. This is an area where we probably, might agree on.

Senator ALEXANDER. I think we might.

The CHAIRMAN. Carolle Fleurio is a cook at a family restaurant near Atlanta, GA. She works full-time to help support her husband who, I understand, is disabled, two daughters, and a granddaughter, and a niece.

Melvin Sickler owns multiple franchises of Auntie Anne's Pretzels—who hasn't had those when you go through airports—and Cinnabon in New Jersey. He is here today testifying on behalf of the National Restaurant Association.

David Rutigliano is a member of the Connecticut House of Representatives, a fellow legislator, and an owner of the Southport Brewing Company Restaurant, which has several locations in the State of Connecticut.

Thank you all for being here. All of your statements will be made a part of the record in their entirety. I read them over last night. They are all very good. We would ask you to sum it up, if you could, within 5 minutes since we have a long panel, and we have a vote coming up in an hour. Now, I don't suppose we will get it all done by then, so we will have to take a break, but we will see how far we can get before then.

With that, I will start from left to right, Mr. Avakian, if you could just sum up your testimony in 5 minutes, and then we will go from left to right.

Thank you, and please proceed.

STATEMENT OF BRAD AVAKIAN, COMMISSIONER, OREGON BUREAU OF LABOR AND INDUSTRIES, PORTLAND, OR

Mr. AVAKIAN. Thank you, Chairman Harkin and Senators for inviting me to share Oregon's successful experience in indexing the minimum wage to the Consumer Price Index.

I am Brad Avakian. I am Oregon's Commissioner of Labor and Industries. In our State, the position of commissioner is a non-partisan, statewide, elected office charged with protecting workers by enforcing civil rights and wage and hour laws, training much of Oregon's workforce, and supporting the success of our Oregon businesses by helping them navigate their way through complicated State and Federal laws.

I am here today to support the committee's efforts in indexing the national minimum wage to the Consumer Price Index, and to offer Oregon's perspective on how we have been able to do that successfully over the last 10 years.

In 2002, our minimum wage was indexed to the Consumer Price Index by way of a voter supported initiative. The effort was supported by seniors, religious leaders, labor. It was supported by both rural and urban counties in our State. And at the heart of the effort was really the principle of basic fairness and smart economics.

We believe that stronger businesses and a healthier economy is achieved when people have the purchasing power to buy the very goods and services that local businesses provide. It is no surprise that minimum wage families are not investing their money in 401(k)'s and mutual funds. Every dime in the increase of the minimum wage is a dime that gets reinvested back into community businesses as people purchase gas, and groceries, school supplies, and the like.

Small businesses, in fact, are dependent on that kind of a local purchasing power. And as inflation causes the price of goods and services to rise, businesses need consumers to be able to keep pace with the rise of the cost of their goods. And so, indexing the minimum wage to the Consumer Price Index is good both for workers and it is necessary for the success of local businesses.

Here is how it works in Oregon. Every September, when we get the new numbers on the Consumer Price Index, we calculate the difference between the new year's numbers and the last year's numbers, and we multiply that difference by our existing minimum wage. And that very simple equation gives you what the increase will be in the minimum wage for that year. If the Consumer Price Index goes down, then our minimum wage stays level. The last thing that we want to do in Oregon is to hurt Oregon's workers by decreasing their wages in a down economy and taking away the ability for local businesses to continue having profitable sales because of that.

The other thing we achieve by linking to the Consumer Price Index is certainty and predictability both for local businesses and for workers. In the last 10 years, we have had no major spikes in our minimum wage. The increases have been steady and they have been predictable.

Even the restaurant industry is doing well in our State. We have nearly 9,000 restaurants in Oregon that employs over 172,000 workers. The National Restaurant Association has stated that the Oregon restaurant industry remains a driving force in Oregon's economy, and that is after 10 years of indexing the minimum wage in our State.

My position of Commissioner in the Bureau of Labor and Industries is in a very unique position in order to monitor the effects of our linkage to the Consumer Price Index.

We get nearly 20,000 calls a year from Oregon businesses. Last year, we trained over 4,000 managers in wage and hour law. I have regular meetings with businesses, business leaders, and chambers of commerce around the State.

Their concern is where they are going to get their good locally skilled workers, not the linkage to the Consumer Price Index and the minimum wage. In fact, a couple of weeks ago, I had lunch with a business owner whose family business, for decades, has been a string of successful truck stops in the State, and he brought up the topic of Oregon's minimum wage and the effort that this committee is considering.

His concern wasn't that the minimum wage was increasing. His concern was that as we erode the middle class and the poorer class expands, where is his family business going to get strong consumers with purchasing power in the future?

Small business survives only if consumers have that purchasing power. American small businesses need it. American workers, which are the most skilled and hardworking on the globe, deserve the raise.

Mr. Chair, I thank you, once again, for your invitation to share our experience with you, and I look forward to your questions.

[The prepared statement of Mr. Avakian follows:]

PREPARED STATEMENT OF BRAD AVAKIAN

Mr. Chairman, Senators. Thank you for the opportunity to discuss Oregon's 10-year history of indexing our voter-passed minimum wage to the Consumer Price Index (CPI).

My name is Brad Avakian and I serve as Oregon's Commissioner of Labor and Industries, a non-partisan statewide-elected position. Our agency protects Oregon's workforce, supports local businesses with technical assistance, and enforces our State's civil rights and wage and hour laws so that workers are protected and responsible employers have a level playing field on which to operate.

We also administer the State's indexed minimum wage law, passed in 2002 by a diverse coalition of labor, senior, religious and hunger security organizations and advocates.

I'm here today to offer our agency's perspective on Oregon's successful experience in administering the measure and applaud Senator Harkin and the committee for raising this important discussion.

After more than 10 years of implementation, we know that Oregon's minimum wage law has been good for workers and businesses. By indexing the minimum wage to inflation, we've made sure that workers don't lose ground as the costs of everyday goods increase. Our system also provides employers with greater certainty and predictability for payroll expenses over time.

Oregon's law is guided by the understanding that increasing workers' purchasing power leads to a healthier economy. Virtually every dime that comes through a higher minimum wage is reinvested in the local economy when the worker buys groceries, gas, clothes, school supplies and other essentials. We know that the price on goods and services will increase with inflation. The success of local business is dependent on customers continuing their ability to purchase by seeing their wage keep pace with the cost of living.

HOW IT WORKS

The Oregon measure directs the Labor and Industries Commissioner to adjust the minimum wage for inflation every September, rounded to the nearest 5 cents. The adjustment accounts for inflation as measured by the CPI, a statistic published by the U.S. Bureau of Labor Statistics to track the average change in prices over time for a fixed "market basket" of goods and services.

For example, in September 2012, Oregon's minimum wage was $8.80. Based on an increase in the CPI of 1.69 percent from August 2011 to August 2012, my office used a simple calculation to determine the rate for 2013:

$8.80 X .0169 = $.1487, rounded to $.15

The administration is simple and straight-forward.

Notably, we have not seen major spikes or steep wage increases year-to-year. The increases have been steady for employers—providing them with a healthy level of certainty and predictability. In fact, the largest wage increase in the decade since voters enacted Oregon's minimum wage law occurred in 2008 with a modest $.45, 6-percent increase.

The following year—as Oregon and the rest of the country struggled with the Great Recession—we saw no wage increase because of the declining CPI. This is an important built-in protection for workers during difficult economic times, and I appreciate the committee's approach in not having a drop in the CPIW trigger a decrease in wages when working families need it most.

PROTECTING ALL OREGONIANS

Notably, Oregon's voter-enacted system also guarantees a minimum wage to wait staff. Our restaurant industry is doing well—we have 8,867 restaurants that employ 171,900 Oregonians across the State. According to the National Restaurant Association, restaurants remain "a driving force in Oregon's economy."

OREGON: OPEN FOR BUSINESS

The Oregon Bureau of Labor and Industries provides technical assistance for more than 17,000 businesses each year. In addition, I frequently travel the State to meet with business leaders and local chambers of commerce.

When I meet with business owners, they ask me about creating a pipeline of skilled workers to get our economy back on track. Oregon's minimum wage is not an issue in those discussions. In fact, the last time that the issue came up in a meeting with an employer, it was in the context of the business owner saying that the Federal minimum wage was too low for workers because it hasn't kept up with the cost of raising a family.

Oregon is a great place to do business. We value our workforce through a minimum wage that ensures that workers' buying power doesn't slip as the cost of everyday essentials rises.

Thank you again for your consideration of this issue and the critical work of protecting America's workforce. I look forward to your questions.

Bureau of Labor and Industries

<u>Wage increases year-to-year have not spiked</u>:

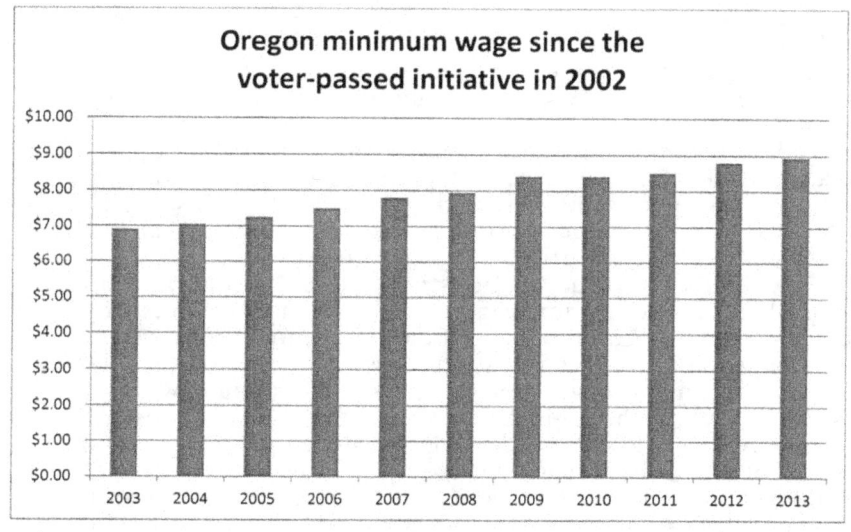

Source: Oregon Bureau of Labor and Industries wage data

The CHAIRMAN. Thank you very much, Commissioner Avakian. Dr. Dube, welcome. Please proceed.

STATEMENT OF ARINDRAJIT DUBE, Ph.D., DEPARTMENT OF ECONOMICS, UNIVERSITY OF MASSACHUSETTS AMHERST, AMHERST, MA

Mr. DUBE. Thank you, Chairman Harkin, and members of the committee for the opportunity to speak here today.

My name is Arin Dube. I am Assistant Professor of Economics at the University of Massachusetts Amherst, and my area of expertise is on labor markets and minimum wages.

As we consider the question of indexation, it is useful to keep in mind that over the past 30 years, the minimum wage has not kept up with the cost of living.

As we heard earlier, adjusted for inflation, the high water mark for minimum wage was in 1968 where it stood, roughly, at $10.60 an hour, and today it is $7.25 an hour.

Under the proposed legislation, with the full adjustment by 2016, I estimate that the minimum wage will likely reach $9.38 in today's dollars. So that's $10.10 when it actually happens, but it is useful to keep in mind that it will be $9.38 in today's dollars in 2016. That is a substantial increase, but it will still be lower than the high water mark back in the last 1960s.

In the longer run, indexation will also eliminate the large fluctuations we have seen in the real minimum wage, which are unattractive for both workers as well as employers. As a result, even some economists who are opposed to high minimum wage policies support indexation. A falling minimum wage has also directly contributed to rising inequality.

Existing research suggests that about half the gap between the middle and the bottom of the labor market that has grown has been due to a falling real minimum wage. The increase followed by indexation will both narrow and stabilize the gap going forward.

How should we think about setting a level of a real minimum wage? Economists often look to the ratio of the minimum and the median wage as a way of measuring the strength or the bite of the policy.

Today, the minimum wage stands at 37 percent of the median wage in the United States. For other developed countries, that ratio is more like 50 percent. We are actually second to last amongst our peers, our ranking ahead only of the Czech Republic.

Back in 1968, that ratio of the minimum to the median wage was at 55 percent of the median. I estimate that the proposed increases will place the minimum wage at right about 50 percent by 2016, close to both the historical and the international norm.

What are the likely impacts on jobs for raising and stabilizing the real minimum wage? For the range of minimum wage increases we have seen in the United States over the past two decades, the recent evidence based on credible methodologies do not find job losses of any sizable magnitude.

I want to be clear that there isn't universal agreement amongst economists on whether there are some job losses following these minimum wage increases. So here, I want to make three points.

First, it is important to keep in mind that the academic debate about minimum wages and jobs is a disagreement over no job losses or small job losses for high impact groups such as teenagers.

Second, studies finding negative impact on jobs like the ones Senator Alexander mentioned, are often not careful about picking control groups, picking up artifacts unrelated to minimum wage increases which could be deindustrialization, technological change, or even weather patterns.

Studies comparing similar areas, neighboring areas right across the State borders, for example, can overcome a lot of these problems. In my own work, we have looked at State borders with dozens of minimum wage increases over nearly two decades and found no impact on restaurant jobs or teen employment. And these results hold, by the way, even when looking at soft labor markets.

Finally, most of studies, surveys of studies and meta studies also suggest that the impact of jobs is small.

So how do economists as a whole, today, feel about minimum wages? The best pulse of the discipline is the IGM panel of 41 lead-

15

ing economists organized by the University of Chicago, my alma mater. When recently asked about whether they supported raising and indexing the minimum wage, the economists supporting the proposition outnumbered opponents by a factor of 4 to 1.

If employment effects of minimum wages are small, what effects can we expect to see? First, evidence shows that for the proposed increase, turnover would fall by about 8 percent or so. This increases productivity as workers stick around longer, reducing training costs.

There would also be some increases in prices in the restaurant sector. For instance, the price of a $1 soda may rise by 2 to 3 cents. But given this relatively small fraction of workers who are minimum wage earners, any impact on the overall price level would be very small, and this is not a controversial claim.

Finally I would argue that the best evidence shows that there are some moderate reductions we can expect in the poverty rate, mostly reversing the increases that took place during the last downturn.

That sums up most of the salient ways in which the economy would actually react to the proposed minimum wage increase.

Thank you, again.

[The prepared statement of Mr. Dube follows:]

PREPARED STATEMENT OF ARINDRAJIT DUBE, PH.D.

EXECUTIVE SUMMARY

1. The minimum wage has failed to keep pace with productivity, while top pay and corporate profitability have grown rapidly.
   - A falling minimum wage has contributed to rising inequality, explaining around half of the rise in inequality in the bottom half of the pay distribution, and more so for women.
   - Raising and indexing the minimum wage would reduce the gap between those at the bottom and the rest of the workforce.
2. Minimum wages have not kept pace with cost of living.
   - Adjusted for inflation, the real minimum wage has fallen from a high of $10.60 in 1968 to $7.25 in today's dollars.
   - Harkin-Miller would bring minimum wages up to $9.38 in today's dollars.
   - Indexation makes the adjustment process much more predictable. Even some economists who are skeptical about minimum wage policies support indexation.
3. Minimum wages have also lost ground in comparison to median wages.
   - The minimum fell from a high of 55 percent of the median wage in 1968 to 37 percent.
   - Harkin-Miller would likely raise the minimum to 50 percent of the median wage—close to the average for other OECD countries, and the U.S. historical norm during the 1960s and 1970s.
4. For the range of minimum wage increases we have seen in the United States over the past two decades, recent evidence based on credible methodologies do not find job losses of any sizable magnitude.
   - The academic disagreements are over no job losses or small job losses for highly impacted groups.
   - While some studies continue to find negative effects, these are often artifacts of regional trends and other factors unrelated to minimum wage increases.
   - Studies comparing similar neighboring areas right across the border account for these problems and find no impact on jobs either for sectors like restaurant and retail, or groups like teens.
   - Employment effects do not seem to vary by the phase of the business cycle or whether the State indexes its minimum wage to inflation.
   - Most surveys and meta-analyses have also concluded that employment effects are small.

- This is why more economists today tend to support increasing and indexing than oppose it—even though there is scholarly disagreement on the precise impact.

5. While employment may not fall from moderate increases in minimum wages, both separation and hires fall, lowering the turnover rate.
   - In the increasingly popular economic models with search frictions, lower quits and layoffs, along with increased search activity by the unemployed, can explain why employment response is small.
   - Lower turnover can also increase productivity.
   - Outside of the simple Econ 101 type environment, increasing workers' pay can improve the functioning of the low wage labor market.

6. Based on existing evidence, we can expect some increases in restaurant prices from a minimum wage increase. However, the overall price level is unlikely to change noticeably, and there is little risk of wage-price spirals from indexation.

7. The best evidence suggests that minimum wage increases lead to moderate reductions in the poverty rate, especially together with the Earned Income Tax Credit.
   - There are strong theoretical rationales—and empirical confirmation—that minimum wages and EITC are complementary policies when it comes to helping low-income families.
   - A high minimum wage prevents wage reductions that can result from an EITC.
   - Since the EITC is indexed to the CPI, minimum wage indexation will prevent erosion of EITC benefits for minimum wage workers.

———

Thank you Chairman Harkin, and members of the committee for the opportunity to speak here today.

My name is Arindrajit Dube, and I am an Assistant Professor of Economics at the University of Massachusetts Amherst. My area of expertise is on labor market policies, with emphasis on low-wage workers. I have done extensive research on minimum wage laws over the past 8 years, as well as research on other types of employer mandates. I welcome this opportunity to share with you findings from both my own research as well as the sizable body of evidence that economists have marshaled on the question of increasing minimum wages.

Today I want to highlight some of the key economic factors to consider when deciding on an appropriate adjustment to the minimum wage. I will discuss how the minimum wage adjustment process has worked in the context of the overall economy, keeping in mind movements in inequality and cost of living. I will specifically consider the role of indexation of the minimum wage to the consumer price index. And I will also share with you what we know about how the economy adjusts to such changes in minimum wages.

I. THE ECONOMIC CONTEXT

A. Rising Inequality

Summary: The minimum wage has failed to keep pace with productivity, while top pay and corporate profitability have grown rapidly.

- *A falling minimum wage has contributed to rising inequality, explaining around half the rise in inequality in the bottom half of the pay distribution, and more so for women.*
- *Raising and indexing the minimum wage would reduce the gap between those at the bottom and the rest of the workforce.*

For much of the past three decades, we have seen a sharp rise in income inequality—fueled by both a rising dispersion in wages, as well as a reduction in labor's share of income. The bottom of the labor market has failed to keep up with overall economic gains.

Wage inequality has grown substantially over the past 30 years, beginning around 1980. As shown in Figure 1, most of this increase has been in the top half of the wage distribution, especially since the 1990s. The only time we saw an increase in the wages of the lower half of the distribution was during the period of low unemployment in the late 1990s. As a result, the 90th percentile real wage grew by over 30 percent between 1973 and 2011, while the median and 10th percentile real wage grew by less than 5 percent over the same period (see Figure 1).

Figure 1: Wages in the U.S. by Percentiles (Index=1 for 1973)

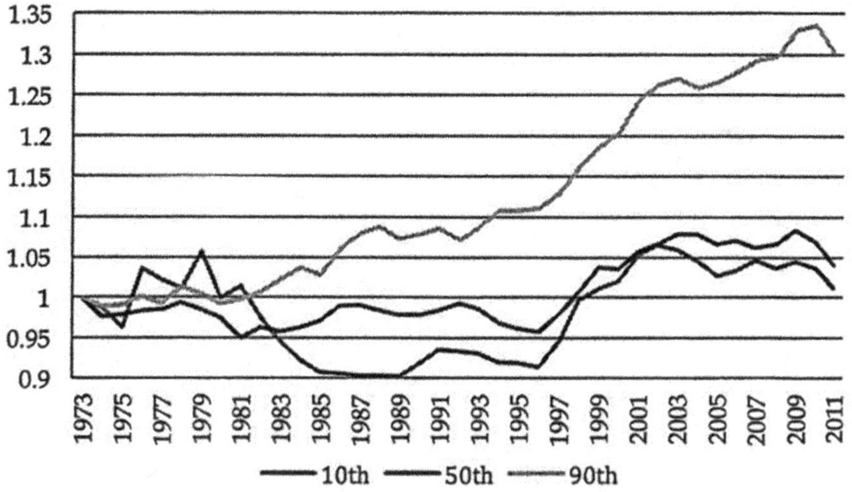

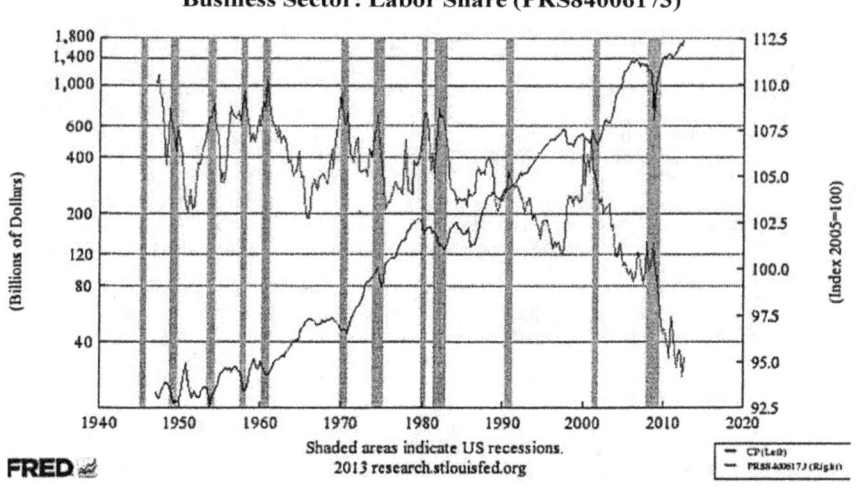

Source: CPS Merged Outgoing Rotation Groups data as reported in State of Working American 2011.

During the past three decades, we have also seen a general downward trend in labor's share of income—interrupted only by the late 1990s boom. The shift toward capital income has shrunk the size of the pie going to workers as a whole. Today, the share of income going to labor as opposed to capital stands at a post-war near-low. Meanwhile, corporate profitability has been growing at a steady clip and has been restored during the current recovery. These two factors—increased wage inequality and a fall in labor's share—have kept those at the bottom end of the labor market from sharing in our economic progress.

Figure 2: U.S. Corporate Profits and Labor Share of Income
Corporate Profits After Taxes (CP)
Business Sector: Labor Share (PRS84006173)

As a way to see how the gap between a minimum wage worker and others in our economy has grown, in Figure 3, I plot how the minimum wage would have changed over the past 30 years had it grown at the same rate as productivity. And how it would have evolved if it had kept pace with the income going to the top 1 percent

18

of the income distribution. For comparison, I also show the actual inflation-adjusted minimum wage (using the CPI–W).

Figure 3: Real Minimum Wages Actual Versus Counterfactual Using Productivity or Top 1 Percent Income Growth

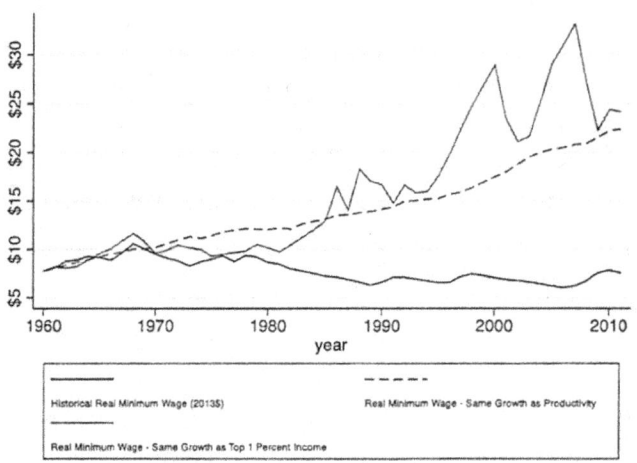

It is quite remarkable that had the minimum wage kept up with overall productivity, it would have been $22 per hour in 2011. Had it kept up with the growth in income going to the top 1 percent, it would have been even higher, at $24 per hour; and the wage would have exceeded $33/hour at its peak in 2007.

This evidence does not suggest that the minimum wage should be increased to $22 or $24 per hour. Rather, the exercise demonstrates how different the growth rates have been for incomes going to those at the bottom of the labor market as compared to the economy as a whole, and to those at the top end of the distribution. Of course, there are many reasons behind this dramatic rise in inequality, including technological change, falling rates of unionization, de-industrialization, increased trade, deregulation and more. And we certainly cannot expect minimum wages alone to solve the challenge of growing inequality. However, there is also substantial evidence showing that a falling real minimum wage has contributed to this growth in inequality.

Lee (1999) was one of the first papers to take a comprehensive look at the effect of minimum wages on wage inequality. He found a sizable spillover effect—whereby the fall in the minimum lowered wages of those higher up in the ladder. He argued that nearly all of the growth in inequality in the bottom half of the wage distribution during the 1980s could be explained by the erosion of minimum wage through inflation. Considering the 50/10 gap—the ratio of the median wage to the wage at the 10th percentile—Lee found that 70 percent of the increase for men, and between 70 and 100 percent of the increase for women, could be explained by the decline in the value of the minimum wage.

A more recent paper by Autor Manning and Smith (2010) uses a more refined methodology, and finds somewhat smaller spillover effects. However, they too find that minimum wages played an important role in determining the 50/10 gap—which is a measure of wage inequality in the bottom half of the distribution. Table 1 below reproduces their key findings, and shows that maintaining the minimum wage at the 1979 level in real terms would have staved off somewhere between half and three-quarters of the overall increase in the bottom-half wage inequality depending on the period in question. Moreover, the minimum wage has a larger effect on inequality for female workers, who tend to be lower paid.

19

Table 1.—Effect of the Minimum Wage on Wage Inequality: The 50/10 Wage Ratio

	Actual	Counterfactual with 1979 minimum wage (2SLS)	Difference	Proportion due to MW (In percent)
A. 1979—1991				
Female	22.40	9.65	12.75	56.9
Male	11.20	9.5	1.70	15.2
Pooled	7.10	1.65	5.45	76.8
A. 1979—2009				
Female	25.20	10.98	14.23	56.4
Male	5.30	5.43	-0.13	-2.4
Pooled	11.40	6.28	5.13	45.0

Notes: Calculated using Autor Manning and Smith (2010) Table 5. The Counterfactuals with 1979 use an average of the two 2SLS estimates reported by the authors.

Both Lee and Autor, et al., use State-level variation in minimum wages over time, and a modeled counterfactual wage distribution, to reach their conclusion. A different approach using decomposition methods such as Dinardo Fortin and Lemieux (1996) and Chernozhukov Fernandez-Val and Melly (2013) tend to find even larger impacts of minimum wage on inequality. The latter set of authors, using cutting edge distributional decompositions find that the minimum wage can explain nearly all of the increase in the pooled 50/10 ratio between 1979 and around 1/3 of the increased standard deviation in log wages (a measure of overall inequality).

To sum up, while there is some scholarly disagreement about the exact magnitudes of the impact of minimum wages on inequality, we know that the decline in the real minimum has played an important role in increasing inequality in the bottom half of the wage distribution, especially for women.

B. Minimum Wages Have Not Kept Up with Cost of Living

Summary: Minimum wages have not kept pace with cost of living.

- *Adjusted for inflation, the real minimum wage has fallen from a high of $10.60 in 1968 to $7.25 in today's dollars.*
- *Harkin-Miller would bring minimum wages up to $9.38 in today's dollars.*
- *Indexation makes the adjustment process much more predictable. Even some economists who are skeptical about minimum wage policies support indexation.*

Over the last three decades, the minimum wage has failed to keep up with cost of living. Figure 4 shows the value of the Federal minimum wage in 2013 dollars spanning from 1960 to 2016—with projected values using the Harkin-Miller proposal. These projections are based on a passage of the bill in 2014, with the full phase in by 2016. I am using the CPI-W to adjust for inflation, and also assuming a 2.5 percent annual inflation rate over the next 3 years (roughly the average over the past 3 years). While the details of the discussion that follows will differ from using a different CPI, or different timing of passage, or different inflation assumptions, the main message would not change substantially.

Figure 4: Evolution of the Real Minimum Wage in the U.S. (2013 dollars)

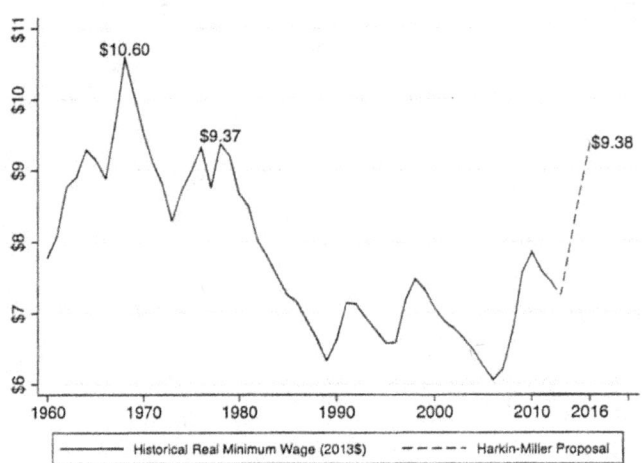

The high water mark for the minimum wage was in 1968, when it reached $10.60/hour in 2013 dollars. The next highest peak was in 1978, when the real minimum wage reached $9.37. During the 1980s the real minimum wage declined to below $7/hour, and over the past 20 years, the minimum wage has largely treaded water, reaching a historical low of $6.06/hour in 2006 prior to the last increase, which brought it to $7.25/hour in today's dollars.

Under Harkin-Miller, with the full adjustment by 2016, the minimum wage will likely reach $9.38/hour in today's dollars. This is a substantial increase, bringing it up to the level in 1978. However, it will still be somewhat lower than the high water mark in 1968.

The fall in the value of the minimum wage has not only increased relative deprivation (inequality), but also increased absolute deprivation. Today, a single parent with one child, working full time at the minimum wage, would earn $14,500 in pre-tax income—below the official poverty line in 2012 ($15,130). With Harkin-Miller phased in, in 2016 her earnings would rise to $18,760. At the 1968 level minimum wage, her pre-tax earnings would have been $21,200. (All these figures are in 2013 dollars.)

Figure 5: Pre-tax Income of Single Parent With One Child Under Alternative Minimum Wages

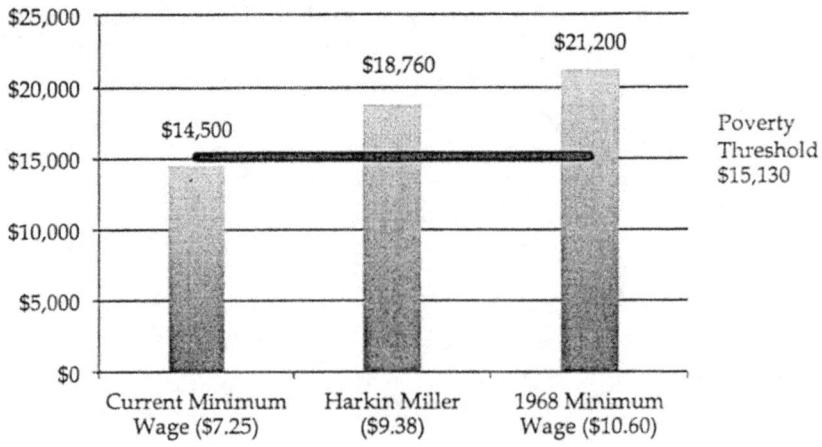

Finally, the sharp swings in the real minimum wage shows some of the inefficiencies of current practices, where the nominal minimum wage stagnates for years, only to be followed by sharp increases. Regardless of what level we set the real minimum wage, pegging it to the cost of living makes it a much more rational and predictable process, which has value to both workers and employers. This is why even some economists who are skeptical about minimum wage policies nonetheless support indexation.[1]

C. Minimum Wages Have Fallen Behind Median Wages

Summary: Minimum wages have lost ground in comparison to median wages.

- *The minimum fell from a high of 55 percent of the median wage in 1968 to 37 percent.*
- *Harkin-Miller would likely raise the minimum to 50 percent of the median wage—close to the average for other OECD countries, and the U.S. historical norm during the 1960s and 1970s.*

When analyzing the strength of minimum wage policies, economists typically use the ratio of the minimum to the median wage, also known as the Kaitz index. There are three reasons to pay attention to this measure. First, a comparison of the minimum wage to the median offers us a guide to how binding a particular minimum wage increase is likely to be, and what type of wage the labor market can bear. Second, a comparison also provides us with a natural benchmark for judging how high or low a minimum wage is across time periods or across countries that vary in terms of their labor markets and wage distributions. Third, the median wage also provides a natural reference group for judging how reasonable a minimum wage level is: most people would not think fairness concerns dictate that the minimum wage should be set equal to the median wage, but they may find it objectionable if it is much lower (say a fourth or a fifth as large). Green and Harrison (2010) argue that voter preferences over minimum wages are likely to track the median wage as an indicator of a reference market wage.

A natural target is to set the minimum wage to half of the median wage. This target has important precedence historically here in the United States. In the 1960s, this ratio was 51 percent, reaching a high of 55 percent in 1968. Averaged over the 1960–79 period, the ratio stood at 48 percent.

Figure 6: Evolution of the Minimum-to-Median Wage Ratio in the U.S.

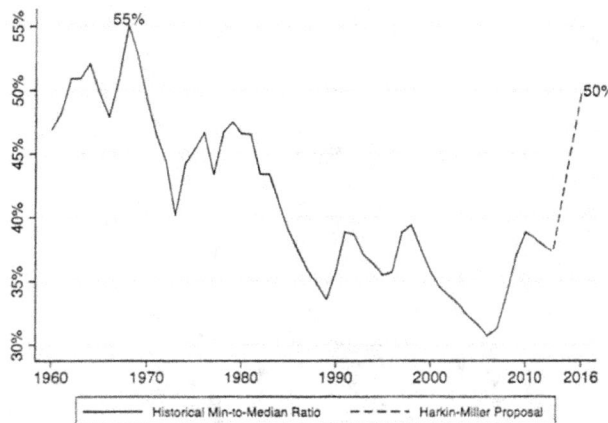

Around half the median wage is also the norm among all OECD countries with a statutory minimum. For this group of countries, on average, the minimum wage in 2011 (latest data available) was equal to 49 percent of the median wage, while averaged over the entire sample between 1960 and 1991, the minimum stood at 48 percent of the median (see Figure 7). It is important to note that many countries

---

[1] Well-known labor economist Daniel Hammermesh, for example, has supported indexation even though he is critical of minimum wages. *http://www.utexas.edu/know/2012/02/09/daniellhamermeshlminimumlwagelelection/.*

such as France and New Zealand today have minimum wages at or close to 60 percent of the median.

In contrast, today in the United States the minimum wage clocks at 37 percent of the median wage, and has the lowest minimum wage in relation to the median of all OECD countries save the Czech Republic (see Figure 8).

Figure 7: Evolution of Minimum-to-Median Wage Ratio in OECD Countries (1960–2011)

Source: OECD Statistics on Minimum and Median Wages

Figure 8: Distribution of Minimum-to-Median Wage Ratio in OECD Countries (2011)

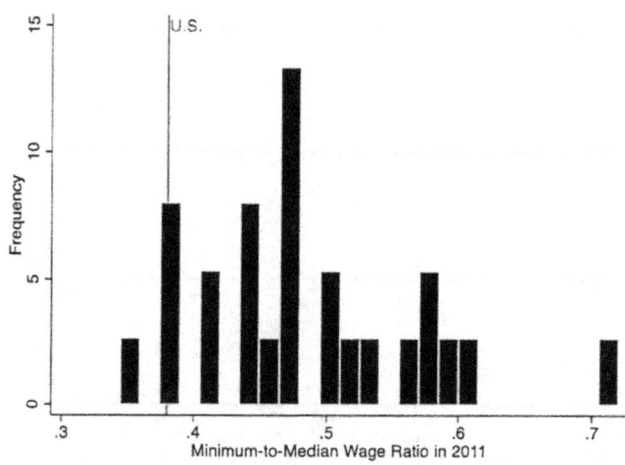

Source: OECD Statistics on Minimum and Median Wages

What would be the impact of the proposed legislation on the minimum-to-median ratio? I estimate that under Harkin-Miller, after the 3 steps have been implemented by 2016, the minimum wage would stand at around 50 percent of the median wage, assuming nominal increases in the median wage at the same rate as the past 3 years. Such a change would bring the United States just above the OECD average and the historical norm prior to the 1980s.

A comparison to the median wage also clarifies why something around $10/hour is reasonable while $20/hour is not. The median wage today is around $20/hour. There are no known cases where the minimum wage was set equal to the median in a capitalist economy. However, there are many cases, including here in the United States, where it was set at or slightly above half the median wage.

II. HOW ARE INCREASES IN THE MINIMUM WAGE ABSORBED?

A. Employment Effects

Summary: For the range of minimum wage increases we have seen in the United States over the past two decades, recent evidence based on credible methodologies do not find job losses of any sizable magnitude.

- *The academic disagreements are over no job losses or small job losses for highly impacted groups.*
- *While some studies continue to find negative effects, these are often artifacts of regional trends and other factors unrelated to minimum wage increases.*
- *Studies comparing similar neighboring areas right across the border account for these problems and find no impact on jobs either for sectors like restaurant and retail groups like teens.*
- *Employment effects do not seem to vary by the phase of the business cycle or whether the State indexes its minimum wage to inflation.*
- *Most surveys and meta-analyses have also concluded that employment effects are small.*
- *This is why more economists today support an increase than oppose it—even though there is scholarly disagreement on the precise impact.*

When it comes to the literature on minimum wages' impact on jobs, it is useful to think of several distinct phases. Until the early 1990s, economists largely relied on time series evidence—correlating changes in the national level unemployment rate for teens to changes in the Federal minimum wage. This older generation literature was shown to have numerous problems, and economists today largely discount these findings today because there are many factors affecting the national unemployment rates for teens that have nothing to do with minimum wages.

Beginning in the early 1990s, a second generation of work (sometimes called the "new minimum wage" research) started exploiting the State-level variation in minimum wages that emerged in the 1980s and grew in the 1990s due to the stagnating Federal minimum wage. The two leading approaches were the State panel approach pioneered by Neumark and Wascher (1992) and case study approach pioneered by Card and Krueger (1994). The State-panel approach used more data, but implicitly assumed "parallel trends" . . . that the low-wage employment trajectories in high minimum-wage States like Massachusetts and Oregon were the same as low minimum-wage States like Texas and Georgia. As it turns out, this is not a good assumption.

In contrast, the case study approach of Card and Krueger (1994, 2000), as well as Card (1992), focused on looking at individual cases with a focus on getting reliable control groups. In their highly celebrated work published in 1994, they found that an increase in the minimum wage in New Jersey did not reduce employment in fast food restaurants in that State as compared to a neighboring State, Pennsylvania. Although these results were questioned by Neumark and Wascher (2000)— who collected their own data—the core findings (lack of job loss) held up when Card and Krueger used official employment data covering nearly the entire workforce using Unemployment Insurance rolls. However, the challenges with the case study approach are that: (1) it is difficult to draw firm inference from single cases, (2) they typically use only a short-time horizon, and (3) results may be difficult to generalize.

Over the past 5 years, we have made a lot of progress in synthesizing the results using these two approaches. The local case study approach has the virtue of using similar controls groups: adjacent control counties are much more alike in terms of observed characteristics than non-adjacent ones (Allegretto, Dube, Reich, Zipperer, forthcoming). This is of particular concern given how regionally clustered high minimum wage States have been over the past 20 years.

In a series of papers with Michael Reich and T. William Lester, we combined the virtues of these two approaches by embedding the local comparisons within a long panels using detailed county level data. In a 2010 paper published in the *Review of Economics and Statistics*, Lester, Reich and I considered *all* adjacent counties straddling State borders for which data was available continuously for the full period between 1990 and 2006—a total of 504 counties. The following figure shows the border counties in the United States.

Figure 9: Map of Border Counties Used to Study Minimum Wage Policies

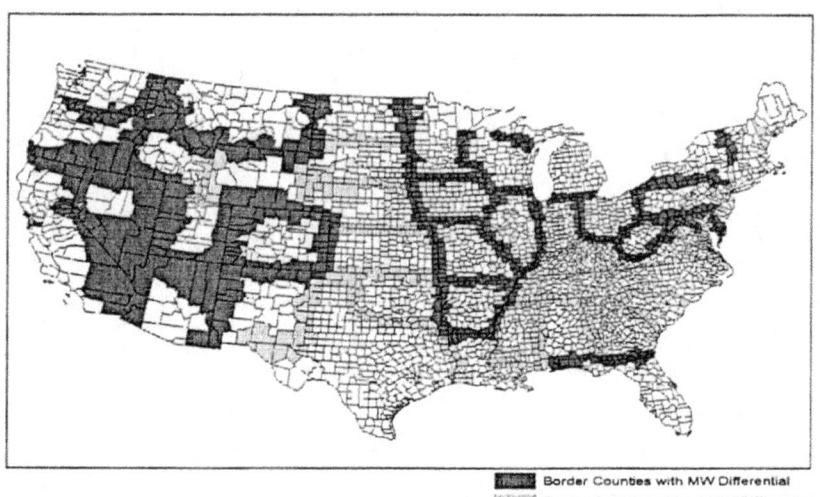

▨ Border Counties with MW Differential
▦ Border Counties without MW Differential

Of these, 337 counties in 288 pairs had some difference in minimum wage. Comparing across these neighboring counties, we showed that there was no evidence of job losses for high impact sectors such as restaurants and retail. This was true even considering four or more years after the minimum wage hike. In followup work, we used the same cross-border methodology to study the effect on teens—a high impact demographic group (Dube Lester Reich 2012). Again, we found no discernible impact on employment. In yet another paper, we used a different dataset and less fine-grained regional controls and again replicated our findings that minimum wages did not reduce teen employment during the 1990s and 2000s. (Allegretto Dube Reich 2011).

Our studies also helped explain why researchers have sometimes found a negative effect on jobs from the policy. Over the past two decades, the variation in minimum wages has been highly regionally selective: the States that have seen greater increases in the minimum wage—typically in the northeast and the west—have tended to be those with lower underlying growth in demand for low-wage workers. Failure to account for these factors will lead us to mistakenly attribute the low growth in employment to higher minimum wages, instead of the real cause (deindustrialization, technological change, bad weather, etc.) For example, we showed that the apparent job losses in the State panel models tend to occur *before* the minimum wage increase occurs, a tell-tale sign of a spurious effect.

In all, we have by now replicated these findings in 4 papers using 5 datasets and 6 different ways of accounting for comparability of areas. These are summarized in Table 2. For high impact groups such as restaurant workers and teens, we find that a 10 percent increase in minimum wage raises average wages or earnings by 1.5 percent to 2 percent. Employment changes are usually close to zero, never more negative than -0.5 percent, and sometimes positive in sign. In all cases, there is clear evidence that minimum wage increases raise total pay going to low-wage workers after factoring in both wage and employment changes.[2]

---

[2] In a very recent paper, Neumark Salas and Wascher (2013), hereafter NSW, criticize our work and question the value of using local controls. By now there is a large body of research that shows why local controls and cross-border research design produce more reliable control groups—including many papers outside of the minimum wage literature. NSW seems to ignore this literature, and instead claim that an alternative technique called ''synthetic control'' picks controls that are not always nearby. However, as we show in a forthcoming paper, they misinterpret their own findings: control States that are within the same census division receive four times as large weights than States outside, confirming that nearby areas are indeed more similar (Allegretto Dube Reich and Zipperer, forthcoming). Moreover, using the synthetic control method, we show that a control State that is 100 miles away on average gets a weight that is seven times as large as a State that is 2,000 miles away—again validating our strategies. Finally, we show that when we use the synthetic control method to estimate the effect of minimum wages on teens using all usable State-level minimum wage changes between 1997 and

Table 2.—Response to a 10 Percent Increase in the Minimum Wage

	(1)	(2)	(3)	(4)
Teens:				
Earnings	1.5 percent*	1.5 percent*	1.6 percent*	
Employment	0.5 percent	1.3 percent	-0.4 percent	
Turnover Rate			-1.9 percent*	
Restaurant Workers:				
Earnings			2.1 percent*	2.0 percent*
Employment			-0.6 percent	0.6 percent
Turnover Rate			-2.6 percent*	
Data Sets:	CPS	ACS/Census	QWI	QCEW
	Allegretto Dube	Allegretto Dube	Dube Lester	Dube Lester
Paper:	Reich (2011)	Reich (2009)	Reich (2012)	Reich (2010)

Notes: Column (1) controls for spatial heterogeneity using census division-specific time effects and State-linear trends; column (2) uses commuting-zone specific time effects; columns (3) and (4) both use county-pair specific time effects. CPS stands for Current Population Survey; ACS stands for American Community Survey; QWI stands for Quarterly Workforce Indicators; QCEW stands for Quarterly Census of Employment and Wages.

Other researchers have also obtained similar results. In independently produced work, Addison Blackburn and Cotti (2009, 2012) found that once they accounted for trends in sectoral employment, there is no evidence of job loss in the retail or restaurant sectors. And that failure to account for such trends generates misleading estimates suggesting job losses. Neither our work (Allegretto Dube Reich 2011), nor others (Addison Blackburn Cotti 2011) found evidence that minimum wages cause more job losses during economic downturns or periods of higher overall unemployment. This is relevant for the current discussion of raising the minimum wage during a time with an elevated unemployment rate.

Since there are 10 States that index their minimum wage to the CPI we can also test whether the employment effects are different in these States. In Allegretto Dube and Reich (2011) we did not find systematic differences in employment response by the States' indexation status.

Leaving the most recent evidence aside, a broader look at the literature also tends to go against the view of large job losses. A review by Charles Brown in 1999 for the *Handbook of Labor Economics* had concluded based on the first round of "New Minimum Wage Research" that employment effects of minimum wages were likely to be small, though the results varied depending on the methods. Similarly, a meta analysis by Doucouliagos and Stanley (2009) concluded that even prior to the most recent work, the literature as a whole (between 1972 and 2007) did not show evidence of job loss. An up-to-date survey of the more recent evidence by Wolfson and Belman (forthcoming) corroborate this finding, and conclude that it was unlikely that the minimum wage increases under study led to statistically or economically meaningful job losses. And when we take into account the demonstrated failings of papers using the State-level approach, this conclusion is strengthened.[3]

While 20 or 30 years ago most economists believed that minimum wage increases invariably cause some job loss, as the data has come in, the profession has updated its beliefs. Recently, the IGM Forum panel of 41 leading economists organized by the Booth School of Business at the University of Chicago was asked their opinion about the desirability of raising the minimum wage to $9/hour as proposed by the President, and indexing it to inflation.[4] The IGM Forum panel is widely seen as representing the pulse of the profession.

Only 34 percent of the economists on the panel agreed with that proposition that the minimum wage hike "would make it noticeably harder for low-skilled workers to find employment." The rest disagreed or were uncertain. It is instructive to compare this with older evidence. Surveys of AEA members in 2000 found 46 percent agreeing with a similar proposition, while surveys concluded in 1992 and 1978 re-

2007, we do not detect any evidence of job losses for teens, with an average employment elasticity close to zero. These findings show that NSW's claims are not borne out in the data, including when we apply their own preferred technique. We also show that the results from one synthetic control case study that found negative employment effect Burkhauser Sabia Hansen 2012, which studies the impact of New York's minimum wage was an outlier.

[3] One review to conclude there is evidence of job loss is Neumark and Wascher (2008). However, as I discuss in Dube (2010), this is a subjective reading of the evidence based on a selective set of papers, and excludes the evidence from the past 5 years. John Schmitt (2013) also provides a useful summary of the key articles, surveys and meta analyses, including many of the ones discussed here.

[4] *http://www.igmchicago.org/igm-economic-experts-panel/poll-results?SurveyID=SV\br0IEq5 a9E77NMV.*

vealed 79 percent and 90 percent of economists agreeing with similar statements (Klein and Dompe 2007). While we should be cautious when comparing across different surveys, the belief that minimum wages necessarily cause job loss no longer appears to be a majority position within the profession.

Even more importantly, overall support for raising the wage and indexing it was strong among the panelists. Forty-seven percent supported the policy, while only 14 percent opposed it, while the rest were uncertain. The IGM panel also reports the responses weighted by the confidence the panelists reported in their answers. Weighted by confidence, the proportion expressing support and opposition were 62 percent and 16 percent, respectively. The third of the panel that expected job losses were split on their support for the policy, while the third that were sure that there would not be job losses were unanimous in their support. (Those who were uncertain broke in favor of an increase.) Today, more economists appear to support a moderate increase in the minimum wage and indexation to cost of living than oppose it.

B. Turnover and Job Flows

Summary: While employment may not fall from moderate increases in minimum wages, both separation and hires fall, lowering the turnover rate.

- *In the increasingly popular economic models with search friction, lower quits and layoffs, along with increased search activity by the unemployed, can explain why employment response is small.*
- *Lower turnover can also increase productivity.*
- *Outside of the simple Econ 101 type environment, increasing workers' pay can improve the functioning of the low wage labor market.*

In contrast to employment levels, there is growing evidence that increased minimum wages reduce employment flows—i.e., turnover. In Dube Lester Reich (2012), we used the same border county methodology to estimate the impact on separations, hires, and turnover rate (turnover rate is the average of the separation and hires rates). We found that for the low-wage groups we considered (teens, restaurant workers), there was a sharp reduction in both separations and hires, even though the number of jobs remained stable. As a result, the turnover rate fell substantially. As Table 2 reports, for a 10 percent increase in the minimum wage, the turnover rate falls by 1.9 percent for teens, and 2.1 percent for restaurant employees, which are substantial magnitudes. In an independent study using Canadian data, Brochu and Green (2012) also find substantial reductions in turnover following a minimum wage increase.

The reduction in separations and hires, concurrent with a steady employment level, offers some clues as to how minimum wages may be absorbed in the low-wage labor market. One explanation is that by reducing frictional wage inequality, an increased minimum wage reduces job-to-job transitions. Put simply, if McDonalds pays a better wage, fewer of its workers will leave to take better paying jobs—say at the higher wage chain In-and-Out Burgers. A higher statutory minimum reduces vacancies at McDonald's, and makes it more likely that the vacancy at the In-and-Out Burgers is filled from the ranks of the unemployed. These two factors tend to help with maintaining the employment level. Second, as Brochu and Green show, a higher minimum wage may also reduce employers' desire to lay off workers in some situations, pushing less people into unemployment.

Overall, even if a minimum wage increase somewhat reduces the number of desired jobs from the employer's perspective, reduced quits and layoffs can compensate and help keep the overall employment relatively stable. Models with search frictions in the labor market—which have become increasingly popular—can help explain this pattern of small effect on employment coupled with larger effect on turnover. Of course this cannot be true at all levels of the minimum wage—with a sufficiently large increase, employment levels will most likely fall as well.

Finally, there are other channels through which minimum wages may positively impact employment. A higher minimum wage can spur those who are unemployed to search more intensely for jobs, as the value of a job rises. It can also bring in workers who previously were not searching because the wage was too low. In models with search friction, job creation is not simply determined by how many vacancies are posted; rather it is a function of both the number of vacancies as well as how many workers are searching for jobs, and how hard they are searching. Generally speaking, workers' bargaining power may be insufficiently low for the purposes of efficiency. By increasing workers' pay, a minimum wage policy can improve the functioning of the low-wage labor market.

There are other implications from reduced turnover as well. Dube, Freeman and Reich (2010) finds that replacement costs are around 8 percent of annual salaries, and are sizable even for blue collar and service workers. Reduced turnover can, therefore, increase productivity through reducing recruitment and training expenses.

These additional channels of adjustment can help explain why moderate increases in minimum wage seem to have small employment effects.

C. Prices, Inflation and Indexation

Summary: Based on existing evidence, we can expect some increases in restaurant prices from a minimum wage increase. However, the overall price level is unlikely to change noticeably, and there is little risk of wage price spirals from indexation.

An additional channel for absorbing a minimum wage adjustment is through increases in the price of the product. The extent to which this occurs depends on how sensitive the demand for the product is to price. Lemos (2008) reviews this evidence, and argues that there is evidence of moderate increase in prices of high impact sectors like restaurants following a minimum wage increase. To date, the clearest evidence on price increase in the U.S. case comes from Aaronson French MacDonald (2008), who find that a 10 percent increase in minimum wage would raise restaurant prices by around 0.7 percent. These estimates would suggest that the proposed Harkin-Miller adjustment would increase restaurant prices by around 2.7 percent. (This is likely an over-estimate because the real minimum wage increase in Harkin-Miller is less than the nominal increase of 39 percent over 2 years.)

While restaurant prices will see likely some increases, the overall price level (e.g., the Consumer Price Index) is unlikely to be noticeably affected by minimum wage hikes. For example, Neumark and Wascher (2008, p. 248) points out:

> "Both because of the relatively small share of production costs accounted for by minimum wage labor and because of the limited spillovers from a minimum wage increase to wages of other workers, the effect of a minimum wage increase on the overall price level is likely to be small."—(Neumark and Wascher 2008, p. 248.)

In a recent op-ed, Aaronson and French (2013) suggest that the overall price level increase from the President's proposal would be around 0.3 percent; analogous calculations would suggest that the Harkin-Miller proposal would increase the overall price by less than 0.5 percent.

The small impact on the overall price level has relevance for indexation. One concern sometimes raised by indexation is that it feeds a wage-price spiral. These concerns stem from the experience in the 1970s, when there was widespread use of escalator clauses in union contracts. However, in the case of minimum wages, the relatively small number of affected workers and the small share of production costs from minimum wage workers limits the scope for feedback into prices. Therefore, worries about "wage price spirals" from an increased minimum wage are misplaced and not typically shared by researchers on the topic, regardless of their opinion about the desirability of the minimum wage.

III. THE MINIMUM WAGE, POVERTY, AND THE EITC

Summary: The best evidence suggests that minimum wage increases lead to moderate reductions in the poverty rate, especially together with the Earned Income Tax Credit.

- *There are strong theoretical rationales—and empirical confirmation—that minimum wages and EITC are complementary policies when it comes to helping low-income families.*
- *A high minimum wage prevents wage reductions that can result from an EITC.*
- *Since the EITC is indexed to the CPT, minimum wage indexation will prevent erosion of EITC benefits for minimum wage workers.*

Minimum wages tend to increase income going to working class and poor families. However, the anti-poverty aspect of minimum wage is limited by the fact that many families under the poverty line do not have substantial attachment to the labor force.

To date, there have been a handful of comprehensive studies of minimum wage on family income, and the evidence is mixed on the strength of the anti-poverty impact. There are some studies that find clear anti-poverty effects (Addison and Blackburn 1999) while others find more small and/or imprecise estimates (Burkhauser and Sabia 2007, Sabia and Burkhauser 2010). However, all of these studies are plagued by numerous methodological problems such as use of aggregate data, lack of sufficient controls, and short time horizons. Many of the estimates are imprecise.

The study with fewest problems is probably Neumark and Wascher (2011), who look specifically at the interaction of minimum wage and EITC on family incomes. Although they do not report an overall estimate for the impact of minimum wages on poverty, their findings show that a 10 percent increase in minimum wages would reduce poverty by around 3 percent for the widest group they studied (18–44-year-old adults and family heads). They find even stronger reductions in the proportion of families with income less than half the poverty threshold.[5] While the impact may differ by particular subgroups, the indication is that minimum wages tends to decrease poverty moderately.

In new work, I find very similar results using a 22-year period and all individuals under 65 years of age. I, too, find that a 10 percent increase in minimum wages would reduce poverty by around 3 percent (Dube, forthcoming). To put this in perspective, this suggests that the Harkin-Miller bill would reduce the official poverty rate from by around 1.8 percentage points, from 15.1 percent to 13.3 percent—a moderate-sized reduction that would mostly reverse the increases in poverty we have seen since the onset of the 2007 recession.

Critics of minimum wages often point to the Earned Income Tax Credit (EITC) as an alternative policy that is better able to aid the poor. However, this is a false dichotomy. The EITC is an important program that likely held the poverty rate down by as much as 1.6 percentage points in 2010.[6] However, a problem with the EITC is that while it encourages work (a good thing), tends to push down wages by increasing supply, passing on some of the taxpayer-funded benefits to employers. EITC tends to lower wages by pushing out labor supply, lowering wages.

Rothstein (2010) shows that after accounting for this leakage, beneficiaries get about 73 cents on the dollar. When we factor in the impact on non-beneficiaries, it suggests that the majority of the EITC expenditures are captured by employers. A minimum wage mitigates this leakage by limiting the wage reductions from an increase in labor supply. Lee and Saez (2012) show how in a wide range of situations, the optimal policy package includes a form of minimum wage and something like EITC. They conclude in that "our results imply that the minimum wage and subsidies for low-skilled workers are complementary policies."

Results from Neumark and Wascher (2011) also indicate that for families with kids (i.e., the primary beneficiaries of EITC)—minimum wage and EITC complement each other in reducing poverty.

Finally, an erosion of the real value of minimum wages reduces EITC benefits for minimum wage workers, since the EITC (unlike the minimum wage) is tied to inflation. The indexation of minimum wages will tend to better harmonize these complementary programs.[7]

REFERENCES

Aaronson, Daniel, Eric French and James MacDonald. 2008. "The minimum wage, restaurant prices, and labor market structure." The Journal of Human Resources, vol. 43, no. 3, pp. 688–719.

Aaronson, Daniel and Eric French. 2013. Spending, income, and debt responses to minimum-wage hikes." Volt. *http://www.voxeu.org/article/spending-income-and-debt-responses-minimum-wage-hikes.*

Addison, John T. and McKinley L. Blackburn. 1999. "Minimum wages and poverty." Industrial and labor relations review, vol. 52, no. 3, pp. 393–409.

Addison, John T., McKinley L. Blackburn, and Chad D. Cotti. 2009. "Do minimum wages raise employment? Evidence from the U.S. retail-trade sector." Labor Economics, vol. 16, no. 4, pp. 397–408; 2011. "Minimum Wage Increases Under Straightened Circumstances." IZA Discussion Paper No. 6036. *http://ssrn.com/abstract=1948032*; 2012. "The Effects of Minimum Wages on Labor Market Outcomes: County-Level Estimates from the U.S. Restaurant and Bar Sector." British Journal of Industrial Relations, vol. 50, no. 3, pp. 412–35.

Allegretto, Sylvia A., Arindrajit Dube, and Michael Reich. 2009. "Spatial Heterogeneity and Minimum Wages: Employment Estimates for Teens Using Cross-State Commuting Zones." Berkeley, CA: Institute for Research on Labor and Employment. *http://www.escholarship.org/uc/item/1x99m65f*; 2011. "Do Minimum Wages Really Reduce Teen Employment? Accounting for Heterogeneity and Selectivity in State Panel Data." Industrial Relations, vol. 50, no. 2, pp. 205–40.

Allegretto, Sylvia, Arindrajit Dube, Michael Reich and Ben Zipperer. 2013. "Credible Research Designs for Minimum Wage Studies." Mimeo, forthcoming.

---

[5] There is only one study that I am aware of that finds a poverty-increasing role of the minimum wage (Neumark Schweitzer and Wascher 2005). They use an unconventional methodology that has not been used before or since this paper, including by the authors. In contrast, Neumark and Wascher 2011 uses standard methodology to estimate impact on family incomes, and tends to find more beneficial results.

[6] *http://www.census.gov/prod/2007pubs/p60-232.pdf.*

[7] *http://www.taxpolicycenter.org/UploadedPDF/311401\Minimum\Wage.pdf.*

Autor, David H., Alan Manning, and Christopher L. Smith. 2010. "The Contribution of the Minimum Wage to U.S. Wage Inequality over Three Decades: A Reassessment." MIT Working Paper. Cambridge, MA: Massachusetts Institute of Technology. *http://economics.mit.edu/files/3279.*

Burkhauser, R.V., and Sabia, J.J. 2007. "The Effective-ness of Minimum Wage Increases in Reducing Poverty: Past, Present, and Future." Contemporary Economic Policy, vol. 25, no. 2, pp. 262–81.

Brown, Charles. 1999. "Minimum wages, employment, and the distribution of income." Handbook of Labor Economics, vol. 3, pt. B, pp. 2101–63.

Card, David. 1992a. "Do Minimum Wages Reduce Employment? A Case Study of California, 1987–89." Industrial and Labor Relations Review, vol. 46, no. 1, pp. 38–54.

Card, David and Alan Krueger. 1994. "Minimum Wages and Employment: A Case Study of the Fast-Food Industry in New Jersey and Pennsylvania." American Economic Review, vol. 48, no. 4, pp. 772–93; 2000. "Minimum Wages and Employment: A Case Study of the Fast-Food Industry in New Jersey and Pennsylvania: Reply." American Economic Review, vol. 90, no. 5, pp. 1397–1420.

DiNardo, John, Nicole M. Fortin, and Thomas Lemieux. 1996. "Labor Market Institutions and the Distribution of Wages, 1973–92: A Semiparametric Approach." Econometrica, vol. 64, no. 5, pp. 1001–44.

Doucouliagos, Hristos and T.D. Stanley. 2009. "Publication Selection Bias in Minimum-Wage Research? A Meta-Regression Analysis." British Journal of Industrial Relations, vol. 47, no. 2, pp. 406–28.

Dube, Arindrajit. 2013. "Minimum Wages and the Distribution of Family Incomes." Mimeo, forthcoming.

Dube, Arindrajit. 2011. "Review of Minimum Wages by David Neumark and William Wascher." Journal of Economic Literature, vol. 49, no. 3, pp. 762–66.

Dube, Arindrajit, Eric Freeman, Michael Reich. 2010. "Employee Replacement Costs." Berkeley, CA: Institute for Research on Labor and Employment. *http://escholarship.org/uc/item/7kc29981.*

Dube, Arindrajit, T. William Lester, and Michael Reich. 2010. "Minimum Wage Effects Across State Borders: Estimates Using Contiguous Counties." Review of Economics and Statistics, vol. 92, no. 4, pp. 945–64; 2012. "Minimum Wage Shocks, Employment Flows and Labor Market Frictions." Berkeley, CA: Institute for Research on Labor and Employment. *http://escholarship.org/uc/item/76p927ks.*

Green, David A, and Kathryn Harrison. 2010. "Minimum wage setting and standards of fairness." Institute for Fiscal Studies London. *http://hdl.handle.net/10419/47492.*

Hamermesh, Daniel. 2012. "The consequences of Romney's proposed minimum wage hike". Know. The University of Texas at Austin. *http://www.utexas.edu/know/2012/02/09/.*

Klein, Daniel and Stewart Dompe. 2007. "Reasons for Supporting the Minimum Wage: Asking Signatories of the Raise the Minimum Wage Statement," Econ Journal Watch, vol. 4, no. 1, pp. 125–67.

Lee, David. S. 1999. "Wage Inequality in the United States During the 1980's: Rising Dispersion or Falling Minimum Wage?". The Quarterly Journal of Economics, vol. 114, no. 3, pp. 977–1023.

Lee, David, Emmanuel Saez. 2012. "Optimal minimum wage policy in competitive labor markets." Journal of Public Economics, vol. 96, issues 9–10, pp. 739–49.

Lemos, Sara. 2008. "A Survey of the Effects of the Minimum Wage on Prices." Journal of Economic Surveys, vol. 22, no. 1, pp. 187–212.

Neumark, David and William Wascher. 1992. "Employment Effects of Minimum and Subminimum Wages: Panel Data on State Minimum Wage Laws." Industrial & Labor Relations Review, vol. 46, no. 1, pp. 55–81; 2000. "Minimum Wages and Employment: A Case Study of the Fast-Food Industry in New Jersey and Pennsylvania: Comment." American Economic Review, vol. 90, no. 5, pp. 1362–96; 2008. Minimum Wages. Cambridge, MA: The MIT Press; 2011. "Does a higher minimum wage enhance the effectiveness of the earned income tax credit?" Industrial and Labor Relations Review, vol. 64, no. 4, pp. 712–46.

Neumark, David, J.M. Ian Salas, and William Wascher. 2013. "Revisiting the Minimum Wage-Employment Debate: Throwing Out the Baby with the Bathwater?" National Bureau of Economic Research Working Paper No. 18681. Cambridge, MA: National Bureau of Economic Research. *http://www.nber.org/papers/w18681.*

Neumark, David, Mark Schweitzer, William Wascher. 2005. "The Effects of Minimum Wages on the Distribution of Family Incomes: A Nonparametric Analysis." The Journal of Human Resources, vol. 40, no. 4, pp. 867–94.

Rothstein, Jesse. 2010. ''Is the EITC as Good as an NIT? Conditional Cash Transfers and Tax Incidence.'' American Economic Journal: Economic Policy, vol. 2 no. 1, pp. 177–208.
Sabia, J.J., and R.V. Burkauser. 2010. ''Minimum Wages and Poverty: Will a $9.50 Federal Minimum Wage Really Help the Working Poor?'' Southern Economic Journal, vol. 76, no. 3, pp. 592–623.
Sabia, Joseph J., Richard V. Burkhauser, and Benjamin Hansen. 2012. ''Are the Effects of Minimum Wage Increases Always Small? New Evidence from a Case Study of New York State.'' Industrial and Labor Relations Review, vol. 65, no. 2, pp. 350–76.
Schmitt, John. 2013. ''Why Does the Minimum Wage Have No Discernible Effect on Employment?'' Washington, DC. Center for Economic and Policy Research. *http://www.cepr.net/documents/publications/min-wage–2013–02.pdf.*
Wolfson, Paul and Dale Belman. Forthcoming. What Does the Minimum Wage Do? Kalamazoo, MI: Upjohn Institute for Employment Research.

The CHAIRMAN. Thank you, Dr. Dube.
Now, to Mr. Prince. Please proceed.

STATEMENT OF LEW PRINCE, MANAGING PARTNER, VINTAGE VINYL, ST. LOUIS, MO

Mr. PRINCE. Thank you, and thanks for the opportunity.

Last year I joined a dozen other small businesses across the table from the President, the Vice President, and several of their economic advisors. The President opened the discussion by asking, ''What can I do to help small business?'' The first of us to speak up said, ''You can raise the minimum wage to $10 bucks.'' I was not surprised. My company has always paid more than minimum wage and my return on that investment has been huge.

My life is a tribute to the American Dream. Senator Harkin gave the numbers on the growth of our business. We started out with nothing and now own a multimillion dollar business with 23 employees.

From day one, we have built this business on wages above minimum. For that small extra investment, I get loyal, long-term employees who are absolutely devoted to my company, and who built ongoing relationships with my customers, and that is what built my business, those relationships.

Senator Harkin gave the numbers on the erosion in the buying power of the minimum wage. When Tom and I started, we never would have believed that 34 years later, the buying power of our customers would have eroded so much, and our lives as businessmen would have been much easier had it not.

If we had indexed the minimum wage to inflation back then, we wouldn't have this buying power problem now. If we had indexed back then, my business would have benefited from my customers having steady, predictable buying power for the ensuing decades. And the businesses that are now having a problem adjusting to a large increase would not have ever had that problem. It would have been a normal cost increase.

For me, good wages are also good business strategy. The last 20 years have been tough on record stores and in St. Louis, two-thirds of the record stores have closed since 2000. Vintage Vinyl has outlasted a 20-store local chain and dozens of national chains. Most of those stores paid only minimum wage. My better paid employees won this life and death struggle for me. High wages made us more competitive.

The crucial part of my job as a CEO is prediction. I project future paths for my company. I make sure we are financially and logistically prepared for them. Part of that is predicting cost. My rent, utility, and health costs always rise, often unpredictably. Indexing the minimum wage would make labor costs more predictable and easier for a business to plan for.

Indexing would especially help businesses that pay minimum wage. They would know exactly what to plan for and exactly when. Indexed raises are gradual and predictable. The 7 years of indexing we have had in Missouri has tacked 85 cents on the minimum wage; that averages out to 12 cents a year. If a business cannot plan for, or absorb, this tiny cost increase, it is already dead and is not going to survive any kind of competition.

Most importantly, indexing makes the buying power of my customers more predictable. Small business owners know minimum wage dollars are spendable dollars and minimum wage earners spend increases right away. Putting a couple of hundred dollars a month in our customers' pockets is a boom to any business. It is a job creator and a business increaser.

Indexing is good for school systems. If wages don't keep up with inflation, neither can rents. The falling return on rental units equals falling property values. Where I come from, schools are financed by property tax.

But most importantly, without indexing, minimum wage earners will fall further into poverty, and this will increase the tax burden on small businesses in an incredibly unfair way. Food stamps, Medicaid, and other subsidies help the needy and it is important that we maintain them. But from a business point of view, when wages are so low that full-time workers qualify for this help, we are actually subsidizing unrealistically low wages that are paid mostly by extremely profitable large corporations. In my State alone, Wal-Mart employees cost Missouri taxpayers $6.5 million a quarter in Medicaid costs. My small business is being forced to subsidize the profitability of my competition. This perverts capitalism and is lousy public policy.

Capitalism and democracy work spectacularly well together because they check each other's excesses. Remember, a $10 minimum will be a floor. It is not a middle-class wage and a paycheck that covers life's necessities is more satisfying to the worker, and encourages that worker to pursue success in our system.

Let's keep the American Dream in sight for those farthest from experiencing its sweetest fruits.

Thank you.

[The prepared statement of Mr. Prince follows:]

PREPARED STATEMENT OF LEW PRINCE

A few months ago I got to join a dozen other small business people across a table from President Obama, Vice President Biden and several of their economic advisors. The business people ranged from a young entrepreneur just starting out to a woman from Detroit whose trucking company had just added its 300th employee. The small business organizations that had suggested some of us for that meeting represent more than 160,000 companies.

The President opened the discussion by asking, "What can I do to help small business?" When the first of us to speak said, "You can raise the minimum wage to 10 bucks," I was not surprised. Because for 34 years my company has always paid more than minimum wage and my return on that investment has been huge.

I co-own and am the CEO of a company called Vintage Vinyl, in St. Louis, MO. My partner, Tom Ray and I started with 300 record albums and a $20 booth at the local Farmers Market. You could say our lives are a tribute to the American dream. We have grown into a multi-million dollar business with 23 employees. We stage 150 in-store concerts a year in our 7,500-square foot store with 40,000 compact discs, a similar number of records and thousands of DVDs. We are the largest independent music store in the Midwest.

From day one, we have built this business on wages above the minimum. For this small extra investment, I get loyal, long-term employees who are devoted to my company; employees whose ongoing relationships with my customers have built my business.

Back in 1979, when we started our company, the minimum wage was $2.90. That would be $9.20 in today's dollars. Even back then, it had eroded from the 1968 level, which would be $10.59 in today's dollars. We never would have believed that 34 years later the buying power of minimum wage workers would actually be lower. That's terrible for small business, terrible for our economy and terrible for our country. If we had indexed the minimum wage to inflation back then, we wouldn't have this problem now. If we had indexed back then, my business would have benefited from the buying power of my customers being steady and predictable for the last 34 years.

I have found that good wages are good business strategy, too. The last 20 years have been tough on the record business. Downloading and free Internet music are killing record stores. In St. Louis, two-thirds of the record stores have closed since the year 2000. We've outlasted a 20-store local chain and dozens of national chains. Most of those stores' paid their employees minimum wage. My creative, loyal, dedicated and better paid employees won this life or death struggle for us. Higher wages made us **more** competitive. While my competition dealt with the costly results of constant employee turnover, constant training costs and the unsatisfied customers that turnover breeds, my employees added value to my business.

Indexing the minimum wage would make it *easier* for businesses to predict and plan for labor costs. The crucial part of my job as CEO is prediction. I must imagine the possible futures for my company and make sure my employees are financially and logistically prepared for them. Part of that is predicting costs. My rent, utilities, supplies and health care costs rise constantly; sometimes unpredictably. Indexing would especially help businesses that pay minimum wage as they would know when and how much to plan for. My bookkeeper and I have already begun discussions in anticipation of your actions.

Indexing minimizes the disruption of rising labor costs in minimum wage businesses because raises are gradual. The minimum wage has been indexed in Missouri since 2007. In that time indexing has tacked on 85 cents. That averages out to about 11.5 cents a year. If a business can't plan for or absorb that tiny cost increase, it's already dead in the water and is not going to survive even the slightest competition.

But most importantly indexing makes the buying power of my customers more consistent and predictable. Small business owners know that higher minimum wages put spendable dollars into the hands of our customers. Minimum wage earners, who live from paycheck to paycheck, spend increases right away. Putting a couple of hundred dollars more a month in their pockets would be a boon to business and a boon to the economy. These dollars go directly to the local grocery store, daycare, or pharmacy. It increases business and creates jobs. It also maintains the local tax base.

Indexing will help government planners. Payroll taxes come from wages and sales taxes come from spent wages. Indexing wages to rise at the rate of inflation can only increase the predictability of revenues derived from taxes related to those wages.

Indexing is good for school systems. The most local small business is landlord. Most rental units are locally owned. The vast majority of minimum wage workers are renters. If minimum wages don't keep up with inflation, neither can rents. When rents fall in relation to the price of other goods, property values fall proportionally and so do property tax revenues. Where I come from schools are funded by property taxes.

Without indexing, people making minimum wage will fall further into poverty, which will increase the tax burden on small businesses and successful individuals. You may think of food stamps, government housing and child care subsidies as helping the poor and they do and it's important that we maintain them. But from a business point of view, when wages are so low that full-time workers qualify for this help, we are actually subsidizing unrealistically low wages paid mostly by extremely profitable multi-national corporations. I feel like I'm being forced to subsidize the profitability of my competition. This perverts capitalism and is lousy public policy, to boot.

For example: In my State, According to the MO Healthnet Employer Report, in the 1st quarter of 2011 (the latest data available) Wal-Mart alone cost Missouri taxpayers $6,506,254 in Medicaid costs. McDonalds cost 3,781,373, Casey's, Dollar General, and Sonic Restaurants cost $1.5 million each, Subway, Wendys and Taco Bell came in at about a million dollars each. That's nearly $18 million of Missouri taxpayer money over eight very profitable, low-wage companies in one quarter.

The combination of democracy and capitalism is a powerful one, but people have to have access to success to buy in. Capitalism and democracy work spectacularly well together because they keep each other's excesses in check. The American Dream isn't functioning when the pie keeps getting bigger, but working people's share shrinks.

A decent wage at the lowest rung lets workers make ends meet while giving them a taste of the rewards of work. Remember, the $10 minimum will be a floor. It's not a middle-class wage. But having a few bucks in discretionary spending or a little more financial stability will make the reward of looking at your paycheck and thinking ''I earned that and it's something to build on,'' a little more satisfying and demonstrate the rewards of work.

Let's keep the American Dream in sight for those farthest from experiencing its sweetest fruits.

In a race to the bottom, the winner ends up at the bottom.

The CHAIRMAN. Thank you very much, Mr. Prince.

Now, we will turn to Ms. Fleurio. Welcome, and please proceed.

STATEMENT OF CAROLLE FLEURIO, RESTAURANT WORKER, JONESBORO, GA

Ms. FLEURIO. Good morning, Senator Harkin, Senator Alexander, and members of this committee.

My name is Carolle Fleurio and I thank you for inviting me to share my personal story. I also want to thank Senator Harkin and all the other Senators who are supporting the Fair Minimum Wage Act, which will not only raise the minimum wage, but guarantee that workers like me will get yearly raises that keep up with the cost of living.

For the last 7 years, I have worked as a cook at a family restaurant in Stockbridge, GA. This restaurant is a place people love to go to. People have meetings there, families come to socialize and catch up with each other. It is a place where people come to feel at home and comfortable while enjoying a meal. Being a cook means that I am the one who helps make this experience possible.

Although I enjoy my job, it's difficult to support a family on $8 an hour. My husband is both retired and disabled, which means he is unable to work. His social security check is barely enough to pay for car insurance for myself and our two daughters—my two daughters, our life insurance policy, and his medical need. My paycheck has to pay for everything else. I am responsible for the mortgage, water, light, garbage, gas, food, and all other household expenses. I provide a home for myself, my husband, my two daughters, my granddaughter, and my niece. I have a family back home in Haiti who cannot find a job. I should be able to provide for them, but I am unable to.

When I started out at this restaurant, I earned $6.85 an hour. I have gotten several small raises. However, the cost of milk and gas keeps going up. Even though I am not getting ahead, these raises keep me and my family from falling too far behind the cost of living. Many people I know don't even get those small raises. That just doesn't seem right.

Some months, my wages just aren't enough to cover our expenses, even though I try very hard to keep our bills as low as possible. I have to make the hard choice on which bills will be paid and which bills will just have to wait. Some months we simply can't pay the mortgage on time. This is very stressful for all of us. My husband and I must keep a roof over the head of all of our family. It takes a toll on our health when we get behind on this important bill.

I am also unable to provide much for my youngest daughter who is in graduate school. She has to work many hours, earning less than I do per hour, to provide for herself. I would love for her to be able to focus on her schooling, or to work fewer hours, so she can study more.

If the minimum wage goes up $1 or $2, that will make a huge change in my life. Not only would it help our family be better able to meet our basic needs, but it will also help when I get sick. I have no paid sick or personal days, so when I am feeling really sick, I have to decide if I have enough money that week to stay home, or if I must go in anyway. With more pay, on those few days a year when I am sick, I could stay home and get better, rather than exposing my coworkers and our customers to my germs.

I have not had a vacation in 7 years, because we cannot afford to go without my pay. With a raise like the one the Fair Minimum Wage Act will provide, I could take a few days off in the year and have some rest time with my family. It's also very important to me that this bill includes an increase every year, to match the rise in the cost of living. That would be a real blessing.

The cost of groceries and utilities goes up every year, knowing that even a small raise is coming will help us plan for these costs. It will give us more security, more peace of mind, and a bit of a cushion for sickness, emergencies, or just the regular expenses of life.

Because I don't get paid time off even after 7 years on my job, I had to think hard about losing a day's pay to come to Washington to speak in support of this bill. I am here today because it is that important for me and my family, and that the millions of families like mine that work hard every day, but still do not earn enough at low-wage jobs to cover the basic necessities of life.

I hope that Congress will pass this important bill. For me, and for the millions of other minimum wage workers around the country, it would mean happiness, joy, and peace.

Thank you.

The CHAIRMAN. Ms. Fleurio, thank you for being here.

Ms. FLEURIO. You're welcome.

The CHAIRMAN. Thank you for putting a real human face on what we are talking about, and representing the millions of people out there that, I have said before, we hardly ever see in our daily lives, but who make our lives better. And these are the people we are talking about here in the minimum wage hearing, so thank you for being here.

Ms. FLEURIO. You're welcome. Thank you too.

The CHAIRMAN. Thank you.

Mr. Sickler, representing the National Restaurant Association. Please proceed.

STATEMENT OF MELVIN SICKLER, FRANCHISEE, AUNTIE ANNE'S PRETZELS AND CINNABON, WILLIAMSTOWN, NJ

Mr. SICKLER. Good morning, Chairman Harkin, Ranking Member Alexander, and the members of this committee.

Thank you for this opportunity to testify today on behalf of my businesses and the National Restaurant Association.

My name is Mel Sickler. I'm a multistore Auntie Anne's Pretzels and Cinnabon franchisee from Williamstown, NJ. I drove from New Jersey to be here today on behalf of small businesses and young people seeking more job opportunities. In that spirit, I ask Congress not to increase the minimum wage.

As I understand it, legislation recently introduced would increase the Federal minimum wage from $7.25 an hour to $10.10 per hour. If this legislation were to become law, it would create a new hardship, particularly on small businesses, at a time that many of us are attempting to contribute to economic job growth in a weak economy.

In 1992 my wife Ginny—who is sitting behind me—and I, after an extensive search of many different kinds of franchises, went all-in financially and purchased our first Auntie Anne's Pretzels franchise. Twenty years later, we own and operate 10 stores in New Jersey. Our growth provides job opportunities for new hires, and creates advancement opportunities for deserving individuals working currently in our stores.

But the restaurant industry was not immune from the effects of the last recession. The industry is now on a rebound and has been an engine of growth for the Nation's employment recovery for the last several years. Restaurants, in fact, have been the third largest private sector job creator since the recovery began in March 2010.

According to figures from the Bureau of Labor Statistics, our industry provides millions of Americans with their first job and critical skills needed for a successful and rewarding career. In fact, one out of every three adults got their first job experience in a restaurant. While it serves as a gateway for many young people to enter the workforce, it also provides easier ways for advancement regardless of your background. Thus, our industry has become very diverse at all levels.

For example, restaurants employ more minority managers than any other industry. An Auntie Anne's crewmember may start at age 16 with no prior work experience, but if my manger sees diligence, pride, and a good work ethic, they quickly raise that young person's wages.

These young workers are eager to enter the workforce and they deserve the opportunity to do so. They deserve the opportunity to start as soon as possible, learning the skills needed to succeed in life that only a job can provide.

The vast majority of minimum wage restaurant workers are young and also not the heads of their household, which probably explains why the average household income of restaurant workers earning the Federal minimum wage is $62,507, again, according to BLS.

Given experience in States that have raised minimum wage above the Federal rate, we know the impact an increase to $10.10 would have on availability of jobs in our industry.

For example, Oregon's State minimum wage is now $8.95, more than a dollar less than what is being proposed. After peaking at 16.4 employees per establishment in 1996, the average number of workers in Oregon's restaurants declined steadily.

The numbers of other States with minimum wages higher than the Federal minimum wage are similar. Food and beverage costs are the two most significant line items for a restaurant, each accounting for approximately 33 cents of every dollar in sales with the average pretax margins of roughly 4 to 6 percent. Increases in food and labor costs can have a dramatic impact on restaurants' bottom line.

While in theory, it may sound to some as a good idea to increase starting wage, the ramifications go further. If I increase the wage that I pay entry level employees by $2.85, then I also have to give a $2.85 raise to my employees that are making $10, $12, $14 and even $16 per hour. Otherwise, it would not be fair to these employees who have been with me for several years and worked their way up the ladder.

I would love to give all of my employees a $2.85 raise, but the reality is I simply can't afford it. In fact, if the starting wage is increased to $10.10, then approximately 75 percent of my employees would end up getting a $2.85 an hour raise. That would result in a 22 percent jump in my labor costs which would be very difficult for my business to withstand. This does not even account for the increased labor—the increase in food, health care, and energy costs which have been rising steadily in recent years.

To handle this negative impact to the bottom line, some will say that restaurants simply need to increase their menu prices, pass the added costs on to the customers. The reality is that I will lose business if I increase menu prices in a challenging economic environment because most of my customers will just not buy from me. Instead, most restaurants will be forced to reduce their employees' hours, postpone plans for new hires and will reduce the number of employees in the restaurant.

Additionally, businesses such as mine will become much more restrained in terms of future growth and expansion. Only a small minority of the restaurants will be able to handle a 39 percent wage increase without taking actions that will harm workers.

I am not a public speaker or care much for politics, for that matter, but I came here to testify because I do not understand why anyone would want to make it harder for small business employers like myself to hire more deserving people. Instead, I would ask you to focus on policies that encourage more people, not fewer, to enter the workforce. Our collective goal should be to get our young people hired and on the path to achieving the American Dream.

With our current 23 percent teen unemployment rate, which is nearly 25 percent in my hometown State of New Jersey, increasing the Federal minimum wage is like throwing an anchor to a drowning man.

The National Restaurant Association looks forward to working with this committee on issues to improve the well-being of our employees without sacrificing their jobs in the process.

Thank you for this opportunity to explain the added burden that increasing the minimum wage would have on my business and the restaurant industry.

[The prepared statement of Mr. Sickler follows:]

PREPARED STATEMENT OF MELVIN "MEL" SICKLER

Chairman Harkin, Ranking Member Alexander, and members of this committee, thank you for this opportunity to testify today on behalf of my businesses and the National Restaurant Association.

My name is Mel Sickler. I am a multi-store Auntie Anne's Pretzels and Cinnabon franchisee owner from Williamstown, NJ. I have 109 employees, 18 are full-time and 91 are part-time employees. I drove from New Jersey to be here today, on behalf of small businesses and young people seeking more job opportunities. In that spirit, I ask Congress not to increase the minimum wage.

As I understand it, legislation recently introduced, The Fair Minimum Wage Act of 2013 (S. 460), would increase the Federal minimum wage rate from $7.25 an hour to $10.10 per hour. Additionally, it would raise the cash wage for tipped employees from $2.13 today to 70 percent of the non-tipped minimum wage. If this legislation were to become law, it would create a new hardship, particularly on small businesses, at a time that many of us are attempting to contribute to economic and job growth in a weak economy.

In 1977, after making a difficult decision to leave the family farm, and a career in farming, I started, operated, and then sold, two separate service businesses. Then, in 1992, my wife, Ginny, and I, after an extensive search of many different kinds of franchises, went all in financially, and purchased our first Auntie Anne's Pretzels franchise. We were looking for a business that we both could be involved in and chose Auntie Anne's.

Twenty years later, we own and operate 10 stores in New Jersey. Not only are the two of us working in the business, but our three children are involved as well. Our business plans for the future are very similar to what they have been from the beginning—slow, steady, deliberate growth by adding more locations. Our growth provides job opportunities for new hires, and creates advancement opportunities for deserving individuals currently working in our stores.

MY SMALL BUSINESS IS TYPICAL IN THE RESTAURANT INDUSTRY

The National Restaurant Association is the leading business association for the restaurant and foodservice industry. The Association's mission is to help members build customer loyalty, rewarding careers and financial success.

Nationally, the industry is made up of 980,000 restaurant and foodservice outlets employing 13.1 million people—about 10 percent of the American workforce. Despite being an industry of mostly small businesses, the restaurant industry is the Nation's second-largest private-sector employer.

We are a unique industry. First, we are dominated by small businesses. More than 7 in 10 eating and drinking establishments are single-unit operations. Overall, the restaurant industry also operates under relatively low profit margins—roughly 4 to 6 percent *before taxes*. I know from experience, which is corroborated by the data, that labor costs are one of the most significant line items for restaurants.

THE RESTAURANT INDUSTRY IS HELPING GET AMERICA BACK ON TRACK

The restaurant industry was not immune from the effects of the last recession, with job losses in 2009 and 2010 representing just the second and third years on record that the industry cut staff. However, the restaurant industry is now on a rebound, with the January 2013 employment level up 8.8 percent from the bottom of the cycle. In comparison, total U.S. employment was up only 4.3 percent from the recession, as of January 2013.

The restaurant industry has been an engine of growth for the Nation's employment recovery for the last several years, according to figures from the Bureau of Labor Statistics (BLS). This trend has been particularly evident during the current recovery from the recession, as restaurants have been the third-largest private-sector job creator since the recovery began in March 2010.

Eating and drinking establishments—the primary component of the restaurant industry which accounts for roughly three-fourths of the total restaurant and foodservice workforce—added jobs at a strong 3.4 percent rate in 2012. As of January 2013, total restaurant employment was 441,000 jobs above its high-point before the recession, while the overall economy was still down 3.2 million jobs from its pre-recession peak.

OUR INDUSTRY GIVES MANY THEIR FIRST START

Our industry provides millions of Americans with their first job and the critical skills needed for a successful and rewarding career. In fact, one out of three adults got their first job experience in a restaurant.

While it serves as the gateway for many young people to enter the workforce, it also provides easier ways for advancement, regardless of your background. Thus, our industry has become very diverse at all levels. For example, restaurants employ more minority managers than any other industry and 50 percent of restaurant owners are women.

Wages in our industry also grow at rates above those of the overall economy, according to figures from the Bureau of Labor Statistics. While an Auntie Anne's crewmember may start at age 16 with no prior work experience, if my managers see diligence, pride and a good work ethic, they quickly raise that young person's wages.

MINIMUM WAGE WORKERS ARE YOUNG AND A SMALL PART OF THE INDUSTRY

A majority of minimum wage workers are employed in industries other than restaurants. According to the Bureau of Labor Statistics, 3.8 million individuals earned at or below the Federal minimum wage of $7.25 an hour in 2011. Of these, 45 percent (or 1.7 million) work at eating and drinking establishments. In addition, 60 percent of the 1.7 million restaurant workers who appear as earning at or below the Federal minimum wage are servers, which means their total earnings are above the minimum wage when tips are included.

Thus, excluding servers, only 340,000 earn minimum wage and 344,000 of restaurant workers appear under BLS data to earn below the Federal minimum wage—jointly representing only 7 percent of the total eating and drinking establishments' workforce in 2011. At the same time, government agencies employ 204,000 workers that earn at or below the minimum wage. Many of those 684,000 restaurant workers appearing in BLS to be earning minimum wage or below also share on tips, so, in reality, they earn more than the minimum wage.

I do understand that there are certain individuals, such as student-learners (vocational education students) and individuals with productive impairment capacity, who can be paid less than the Federal minimum wage of $7.25, as is the case with young people for the first 90 calendar days after they are first employed. However, I do not go lower than the minimum wage for any of my employees, including teenagers during their first 90 days of employment. My approach is also the common practice in the industry, as the numbers attest.

Still, it is not hard to understand why Congress would create these incentives for employment at less than the minimum wage for some categories of workers to prevent the loss of employment opportunities for these individuals. In fact, even unpaid entry-level work can be valuable, as is the case with most congressional internships. Young workers at minimum wage in the restaurant industry are gaining valuable entry-level experience—while being compensated for it.

MY CREWMEMBERS DESERVE A CHANCE TO BE IN THE LABOR MARKET

These young workers, who, if they're like my typical crewmember, are eager to enter the workforce. And they deserve the opportunity to do so. They deserve the opportunity to start as soon as possible, learning the skills needed to succeed in life that only a job can provide.

The vast majority of minimum wage restaurant workers are young. Forty-six percent of Federal minimum wage restaurant workers are teenagers, while 70 percent are under the age of 25—most of them, 80 percent, working part-time. The majority of restaurant workers who earn the Federal minimum wage are also not the heads of their households, which probably explains why the average household income of restaurant workers earning the Federal minimum wage is $62,507, according to BLS data.

HIGHER MINIMUM WAGE MEANS FEWER JOBS

Given the experience in States that have raised their minimum wages above the Federal rate, we know the impact The Fair Minimum Wage Act of 2013 would have, if enacted, on the availability of jobs in my industry.

For example, Oregon's State minimum wage is now $8.95, more than a dollar less than what is being proposed in The Fair Minimum Wage Act of 2013. After peaking at 16.4 employees per establishment in 1996, the average number of workers in Oregon's restaurants declined steadily.

By 2011, Oregon's restaurants employed an average of only 13.8 workers, or 2.6 fewer employees than they did before the State's minimum wage began rising above the Federal level in 1997, according to analysis of data from the Bureau of Labor Statistics.

In comparison, as shown in the following chart, all restaurants in the United States employed an average of 16.9 workers in 2011, unchanged from the 1996 level. If Oregon's average staffing levels had remained at its 1996 level of 16.4 employees per establishment, the State's restaurant industry would have employed an additional 23,500 individuals by 2011. This result in other States with minimum wages higher than the Federal minimum wage is similar.

Number of Employees Per Restaurant in Oregon Steadily Declined After the State Minimum Wage Rose Above the Federal Level Beginning in 1997

Number of Employees Per Eating & Drinking Place Establishment: Oregon vs. U.S. National Average

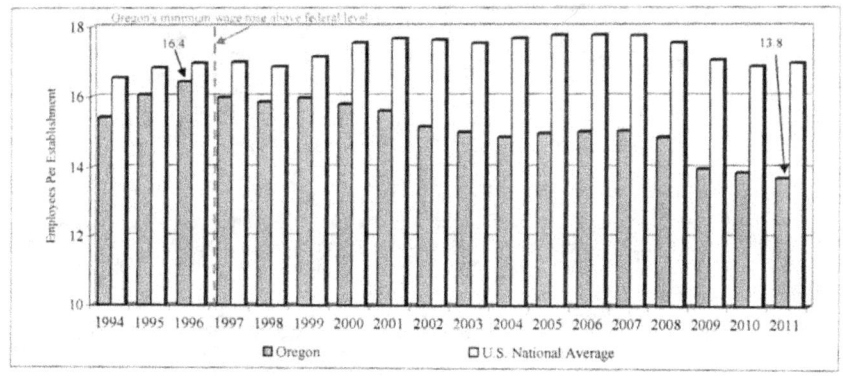

Source: National Restaurant Association analysis of Bureau of Labor Statistics data

TIPPED EMPLOYEES ARE WELL COMPENSATED

Due to our business model, I do not have tipped employees, but because The Fair Minimum Wage Act of 2013 would also increase the cash wage for tipped employees from $2.13 today to 70 percent of the non-tipped minimum wage, I would like to offer some data on behalf of the National Restaurant Association.

On a national level, the median hourly earnings of waiters and waitresses range from $16 for entry-level servers to $22 for more experienced servers. Median hourly tips received by waiters and waitresses range from $12 for entry-level servers to $17 for more experienced servers. The median hourly employer-paid wage ranges from $4 for entry-level servers to $5 for more experienced servers. Thus, once again, it seems that this legislation is a solution in search of a problem that does not exist.

Median Hourly Earnings of Waiters and Waitresses
United States

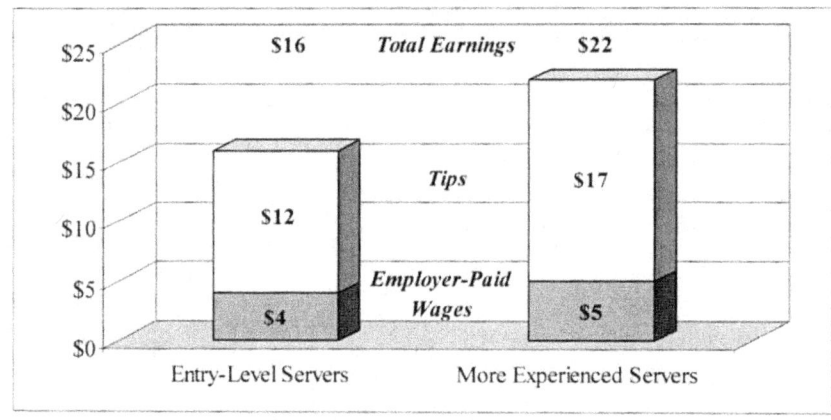

Source: National Restaurant Association, December 2011 Survey

BOTTOM LINE IMPACT OF AN INCREASE IN THE MINIMUM WAGE

Food and labor costs are the two most significant line items for a restaurant, each accounting for approximately 33 cents of every dollar in sales. With average pretax margins of roughly 4 to 6 percent, increases in food and labor costs can have a dramatic impact on a restaurant's bottom line.

Like many other business owners, I am preparing for the impact that the new healthcare employer mandates will have on my business. In fact, I am still trying to figure out whether I have 50 full-time equivalents, which is what would trigger most of the penalties and employer mandates. If a 39 percent minimum wage increase is added to this burden, my labor costs will soar.

The chart below illustrates the impact that an increase in the Federal minimum wage from $7.25 to $10.10 would have on a restaurant's bottom line—not considering any additional costs from the new healthcare law.

While, in theory, it may sound to some as a good idea to increase the starting wage, the ramifications go much further. If I increase the wage that I pay entry level employees by $2.85, then I also have to give a $2.85 raise to my employees that are making $10, $12, and even $14 an hour. Otherwise, it would not be fair to these employees who have been with me for several years and worked their way up the ladder.

I would love to give all of my employees a $2.85 raise, but the reality is I simply cannot afford it. In fact, if the starting wage was increased to $10.10, then, approximately, 75 percent of my employees would end up getting a $2.85 an hour pay increase. That would result in a 22 percent jump in my labor costs, which would be very difficult for my business to withstand.

As a result of a 22 percent increase in labor costs, pre-tax income plunges 58 percent for an average restaurant operation. Prior to the minimum wage increase, pretax income represented 4.4 percent of sales for an average restaurant, or $39,500, in the example below. After factoring in the sharp increase in labor costs, pre-tax income fell to only 1.7 percent of sales, or $16,500.

This analysis does not even account for any increases in food, health care, or energy costs, which have been rising steadily in recent years. It would only take a 6 percent increase in food costs for the pre-tax profit to turn into a loss. This is a likely scenario, as wholesale food prices jumped 16 percent in the last 3 years, according to the Bureau of Labor Statistics.

To handle this negative impact to the bottom line, some will say that restaurants simply need to increase their menu prices and pass the added costs on to their customers. The reality is that I will lose business if I increase menu prices in this challenging economic environment, because most of my customers will just not buy from me.

And as the chart below shows, even a 5 percent increase in menu prices will not be enough to account for such a sharp increase in labor costs. That assumes that a 5 percent menu price increase would even be possible, which according to the Bureau of Labor Statistics hasn't happened since 1982.

Instead, most restaurants will be forced to reduce their employees' hours, postpone plans for new hiring, and/or reduce the number of employees in their restaurants. Additionally, businesses, such as mine, will become much more restrained in terms of future growth and expansion. Only a small minority of restaurants will be able to handle a 39 percent minimum wage increase without taking actions that will harm workers.

Bottom Line Impact of an Increase in the Federal Minimum Wage to $10.10 *

Typical Restaurant With Annual Sales of $900,000

	Before	Public policy impact	After
Income			
Food and Beverage Sales	$900,000	Menu Prices (up) 5%	$945,000
Expenses			
Cost of Food & Beverage Sales	$288,000	Food Costs (up) ??	$288,000
Salaries, Wages & Benefit	306,000	Labor Costs (up) 22%	374,000
Utility Costs	31,500	Energy Costs (up) ??	31,500
Restaurant Occupancy Costs	63,000		63,000
General/Administrative Expenses	27,000		27,000
Other Expenses	145,000		145,000
Total Expenses	$860,500		$928,500
Pre-Tax Income	$39,500	Pre-Tax Income (down) 58%	$16,500
(Percent of Total Sales)	4.4%		1.7%

Source: National Restaurant Association calculations.
Also includes an increase in the cash wage for tipped employees to 70 percent of the Federal minimum wage.

WHY MAKE IT HARDER FOR ME TO GIVE YOUNG PEOPLE A CHANCE TO WORK?

My managers and I are hearing from more people seeking work these days. And I am not a public speaker or care much for politics, but I came here to testify because I do not understand why anyone would want to make it harder for small employers like myself to hire more deserving people. Instead, I would ask you to focus on policies that encourage more people, not fewer, to enter the workforce. Our collective goal should be to get our young people hired and on the path to achieving the American Dream.

With our current 23 percent teen unemployment rate, which is nearly 25 percent in my home State of New Jersey, increasing the Federal minimum wage is like throwing an anchor to a drowning man. The National Restaurant Association looks forward to working with this committee and all of Congress on issues to improve the well-being of our employees without sacrificing their jobs in the process.

Thank you for this opportunity to explain the added burden that increasing the minimum wage would have on my business, and the restaurant industry.

The CHAIRMAN. Thank you very much, Mr. Sickler for——

Mr. SICKLER. Thank you.

The CHAIRMAN [continuing]. Driving this long distance and for your testimony.

Now, we will followup with Mr. Rutigliano.

STATEMENT OF DAVID RUTIGLIANO, OWNER, SOUTHPORT BREWING COMPANY, TRUMBULL, CT

Mr. RUTIGLIANO. Good morning, Chairman Harkin, Ranking Member Alexander, and Senator Warren.

I testify today on behalf of my restaurants and the Connecticut Restaurant Association. My name is David Rutigliano and I am a partner in the SBC Restaurant Group. We started in 1996 and now have six locations along the Connecticut shoreline. After 17 years in business, we employ approximately 250 full- and part-time employees.

At SBC, we are Connecticut. I have two business partners. We are all born and raised in Connecticut. We all got married and started families in Connecticut, and it is Connecticut where we decided to start our businesses.

We want our State, and our country, to succeed and prosper. However, we do not believe Senate bill 460 is the right avenue to achieve this prosperity.

Your proposal seeks to increase the Federal minimum wage by 39.3 percent. In addition, it seeks to increase the cash wage, or tip wage, for tipped employees from $2.13 to $7.07 per hour. This is an outstanding 232 percent increase.

These numbers, simply put, are staggering. At a time when many businesses are struggling to keep their doors open, mandating a wage increase will only hurt those employees in which this proposal seeks to help.

In my home State of Connecticut, we already have the fourth highest minimum wage at $8.25, and one of the highest tipped wages at $5.69. There is a current proposal in our State legislature which seeks to increase minimum wage yet again and also index to inflation. This, along with the recently enacted mandatory Paid Sick Leave law, has contributed to Connecticut being rated at the bottom for business climate and job growth nationally. We also have a persistently high unemployment rate above the national average.

If you add to this the looming Affordable Care Act, I ask anyone here to please explain to us in the restaurant industry, which is labor heavy and low margin, how we are going to afford this mandate.

To be specific, in Connecticut, this bill would add roughly $2,800 per year to the cost of a full-time tipped employee. In other States, it would add as much as $10,000 annually to the cost. These increases will only diminish the amount of opportunity for our young people.

The question of whether an employer can bear the cost of the increased minimum wage should be discussed on its merits, not on scare tactics or appeals to emotion. As a businessman, I have a fiduciary responsibility to my creditors, my family, and my employees to remain profitable no matter what. If an additional mandate means that I will be forced to scale back, then employees could actually be worse off after this passes.

Simply put, increasing the cost of labor means employees are even less likely to hire especially in this down economy. At SBC, we value our employees. Our servers and bartenders work hard. They receive tips and therefore are compensated well above the minimum wage, most making upwards of $20 to $25 an hour, which is fully taxable income.

A mandated increase in server wages only limits the amount of money available for wage increases for other employees like support staff and our culinary staff.

The unemployment rate amongst our young people hovers around 25 percent. An increase to the minimum wage will only increase this number. The minimum wage in my opinion, is meant to be a learning wage.

I do understand the arguments for a living wage. I submit to you that the way to get there should be through a learning wage. By raising the minimum wage, you will be robbing our young people of the opportunity to gain valuable experience and job training.

I understand not all people who work for the minimum wage are young people, but there are other alternatives. We have the earned income tax credit. These are programs that could help these workers without reducing jobs.

Wage mandates are an ineffective way to reduce poverty and cause restaurant operators to make difficult decisions including the possibility of eliminating jobs, cutting staff hours, and increasing prices. These decisions end up hurting the very people that the wage increase is intended to help. This proposal will undoubtedly have a negative effect on thousands of small businesses and employees in Connecticut and across the country.

I urge you to reject this proposal. Any mandated increase to cost will damage an already fragile industry.

I thank you for the opportunity to speak today. I am available for any questions.

Thank you.

[The prepared statement of Mr. Rutigliano follows:]

PREPARED STATEMENT OF DAVID RUTIGLIANO

Chairman Harkin, Ranking Member Alexander, and members of this committee, thank you for the opportunity to testify today on behalf of my restaurants and the Connecticut Restaurant Association. My name is David Rutigliano and I am a partner in the SBC Restaurant Group, a company with six locations along the shoreline in Connecticut. We have been in business for 16 years and employ approximately 250 full- and part-time employees.

At SBC, we are Connecticut. I have two business partners and we were all born and raised in Connecticut. We all got married and started families in Connecticut and Connecticut is where we decided to start our business. We want our State and our country to succeed and prosper. However, we don't believe The Fair Minimum Wage Act of 2013 (S. 460) is the right avenue to achieve that prosperity.

This proposal seeks to increase the Federal minimum wage from $7.25 per hour to $10.10 per hour. That equates to a 39.3 percent minimum wage increase. In addition, it seeks to increase the cash wage for tipped employees from $2.13 per hour to $7.07 per hour, a 232 percent increase. These numbers are, simply put, staggering. At a time when many businesses are struggling to keep their doors open and in some cases employers are foregoing their own paychecks to avoid laying off employees, mandating wage increases will only hurt those employees which this proposal seeks to help.

In my home State of Connecticut, where we already have the fourth highest minimum wage at $8.25 and one of the highest tipped wages at $5.69, there is currently a proposal in the State legislature which seeks to increase the minimum wage to $9.75 and the tipped wage to $6.73. That, along with the recently enacted mandatory paid sick leave law, is making an already difficult situation even worse. Add to that the Affordable Care Act, and I ask anyone here to explain how those of us in the restaurant industry, which is labor-heavy and runs on extremely low profit margins, will survive, let alone prosper, should these proposals become law.

To be specific: In Connecticut, this bill would add roughly $2,800 per year to the cost of a full-time tipped employee. In other States, it would add as much as $10,000 to the annual cost of that employee. In an industry that just earns roughly $2,600 in profit for each employee, an increase of this magnitude just isn't feasible.

The question of whether employers can bear the costs of increased minimum wages should be discussed on the merits, not on scare tactics or appeals to emotion. If an additional mandate means that employers like me will be forced to scale back, then employees could actually be worse off after it passes.

This is what the academic research suggests. Economists from the University of California-Irvine and Federal Reserve Board published the results of a comprehensive review of all research conducted over the last 20 years on the effects increases to the minimum wage had on employment rates. They found that 85 percent of all credible studies came to the same conclusion: increases in the minimum wage are almost always followed by a reduction in the number of jobs—particularly entry-level jobs. Simply put, increasing the cost of labor means employers are even less likely to hire—especially in a down economy.

We value our employees, and they're compensated well. Our servers and bartenders work hard, receive tips and are therefore compensated well above the minimum wage, some making upwards of $20–$25 per hour. A mandated increase in server wages only limits the amount of money left over for wage increases for other employees, like those working in the kitchen.

The unemployment rate amongst our young people hovers around the 25 percent range. An increase in the minimum wage will only increase that number. The minimum wage is meant to be a learning wage. It is meant to give people the opportunity to gain experience and job training. When government increases the cost of labor, employers typically respond by reducing the number of entry-level, low-skilled workers they hire. I understand that not all people who work at the minimum wage are young people, but there are other alternatives—like the Earned Income Tax Credit—that can help these workers without reducing jobs.

Wage mandates are an ineffective way to reduce poverty and cause restaurant operators to make very difficult decisions, including the elimination of jobs, cutting staff hours, or increasing prices. These decisions end up hurting the very employees that wage increases are meant to help. This proposal will undoubtedly have a negative effect on hundreds of small businesses and employees in Connecticut and across the country. I urge you to reject this proposal. Any mandated increase to costs will damage an already fragile industry.

Thank you for the opportunity to testify today. I'm available for any questions.

The CHAIRMAN. Thank you. Thank you very much, Mr. Rutigliano.

Mr. RUTIGLIANO. You're doing great.

[Laughter.]

The CHAIRMAN. All right. I'm getting there. Thank you very, very much. Thank you all. We will begin a round of 5-minute questions.

I think this sort of illustrates the discussion that we are probably going to be having on this over the next few weeks and months, perhaps, here in the Congress; job loss hurting small business.

Mr. Sickler mentioned Oregon, and since we have someone here from Oregon, I will ask you to respond to that. I guess it was Mr. Sickler. I underlined it. Yes, he said that Oregon State minimum wage is now $8.95. Is that correct?

"After peaking at 16.4 employees per establishment in 1996, the average number of workers in Oregon's restaurants declined steadily. By 2011, Oregon's restaurants employed an average of only 13.8 workers, or 2.6 fewer than they did before the State's minimum wage began rising above the Federal level."

Pointing out that if Oregon's average staffing levels had remained at its 1996 level of 16.4 employees per establishment, the State's restaurant industry would have employed an additional 23,500 individuals by 2011.

How do you respond to that, Mr. Avakian?

Mr. AVAKIAN. Mr. Chairman, thank you for the question.

You are right, our minimum wage is $8.95 an hour, and I appreciate the gentleman's comments, but the implication that the job loss is related to the minimum wage simply is not accurate for our State.

Oregon traditionally has a higher unemployment rate than many other States do. We are often one of the first States during a recession to lose jobs and one of the last to bring them back. Over the last 10 years, that has not been related to our indexing to the minimum wage.

What it is related to is our dependence on timber, agriculture, and the high tech industry, which are three industry sectors that oftentimes are hit harder than others during a recession. And that is more indicative of why we end up with job losses.

We are fortunate to have had a minimum wage that has allowed our lowest wage earners to continue pumping what has been, just in the last increase of 15 cents an hour, more than $23 million into our local economies while some of those industry sectors were suffering.

The CHAIRMAN. So you are pointing to the recent downturn in the economy, basically, as a bigger factor than the raise in the minimum wage, which you have indexed since 2002, is that right?

Mr. AVAKIAN. Mr. Chairman, the law was passed in 2002. We began indexing in 2003, and certainly over the last 10 years, there have been ups and downs in markets across the country.

The CHAIRMAN. Right. Right.

Dr. Dube, I want to turn to you because I read through your testimony last night, and it is obviously accompanied by a lot of statistics and charts, some of which I probably do not understand that thoroughly.

But I would like to ask for your input and your thoughts on this idea that increasing the minimum wage causes job losses. What have your studies shown?

Mr. DUBE. I think it is useful to use the Oregon example, and it is also useful to keep in mind that correlations are not always causations, as the saying goes. Minimum wages may be correlated with a lot of things. In fact, it turns out they are correlated with temperature.

Now, I don't think most people would argue the minimum wage causes cold weather, but most minimum wage States actually happen to have colder weather. Similarly, an example with timber and other industries show that it is really important to make apples to apples comparison. You don't want to just compare a State that has a high minimum wage and compare it with the rest of the country without taking into account its industrial structure and other factors, and demographic characteristics as well.

What we did is to look at, for instance, those counties in Oregon border, compare them with either Washington, or Idaho, or California and do this over a 20-year period. To have places that are pretty similar, depend on the same kind of industries, have similar demographic characteristics, and follow them over many years after these increases in the minimum wage and this includes, by the way, the increase in Oregon's minimum wage.

We found absolutely no evidence that the kind of minimum wages that we have seen in the last 20 years, when we have had a lot of variation across the land in the minimum wages, have caused any job losses for low-wage sectors or for groups such as teens.

The CHAIRMAN. So you took contiguous counties, let me understand this, in Oregon that were on the border with a county in Washington, or Idaho, or California. And over 20 years compared the two counties in terms of their minimum wage and job losses in those two counties.

Mr. DUBE. Exactly.

The CHAIRMAN. Contiguous counties.

Mr. DUBE. Contiguous counties. The thing that economists spend a lot of time doing is figuring out how to have credible comparison groups, control groups. We don't have laboratories, we have observational data and need ways to make credible comparisons to make sure that we have the right counterfactual, as the word goes.

What we did in our study, and others have as well, is to compare really similar areas just across the State line. The Oregon example is one, and Connecticut, for instance, comparing Connecticut with the counties right across Massachusetts' border, so that, again, you are making comparisons that are fairly similar.

These counties track each other prior to the minimum wage increase. That makes us reassured that these are good comparison groups, and then we can ask the question: what happens when on one side of the border you saw the increase in the minimum wage and the other side didn't? Then you don't end up making comparisons across places that depend on timber versus that don't, and so on and so forth. And again, we did not find evidence that from the kind of minimum wage increases we have seen there have been job losses.

I am going to be really clear. Does that mean that you can raise minimum wage to any level and that the same conclusions will obtain? Absolutely not. Right? But the point is for the kind of minimum wage we have seen in the United States, historically we can get back to those without necessarily causing job losses.

The CHAIRMAN. Thank you, Dr. Dube.

Senator Alexander.

Senator ALEXANDER. Thanks, Mr. Chairman.

Mr. Rutigliano, thank you for being here today.

Mr. RUTIGLIANO. Thank you.

Senator ALEXANDER. Thanks to all of you for being here today.

Dr. Dube mentioned Connecticut and made comparisons. It seems to me the best way of getting an effect of what might happen is, rather than an academic study, would be to go to somebody running a store and ask what has happened or what will happen. How many stores do you have?

Mr. RUTIGLIANO. We have six.

Senator ALEXANDER. And how many employees do you have?

Mr. RUTIGLIANO. About 250.

Senator ALEXANDER. OK. Now, if you have 250 employees and you were to have an increase in the cost of labor of 39 percent, what would be the——

Mr. RUTIGLIANO. Well, you would reduce employment, or raise prices, or both.

Senator ALEXANDER. What would happen if you raised prices?

Mr. RUTIGLIANO. Typically, we find that our stores vary in counties, we would see a reduction in business in certain parts of the State where we are located.

Senator ALEXANDER. What are your plans for the new health care law coming in 2014?

Mr. RUTIGLIANO. I am on my third Webinar from industry associations honestly trying to figure out how to handle it.

Senator ALEXANDER. But your choice will be to offer more expensive health insurance or pay a $2,000 penalty per employee, or reduce the number of employees, or try part-time employees, correct?

Mr. RUTIGLIANO. Correct.

Senator ALEXANDER. In addition to that, then you would have a 39 percent increase in the cost of employees.

Mr. RUTIGLIANO. Correct. The real increase for us is with the cash wage, the tip wage. This is what we determined to be the most unfair aspect of this. We already pay servers, tipped employees, $5.69 an hour in Connecticut, which is one of the highest in the Nation.

By law, they have to make at least the minimum wage, including tips. On average, they are at $20–$25 an hour. It is almost an unfair increase for this sector of our employees, whereas other employees would suffer for the lack of money available to the fund.

I want to address the doctor for just 1 second. They make it seem like there's consensus on the reports, on the studies, through universities.

The University of California at Irvine and the Federal Reserve Board did their own study. They studied the studies, and they came up with the conclusion that 85 percent of the studies reflect a decrease in employment after the minimum wage. So there is not a minimum wage increase. There is not consensus on the issue.

Senator ALEXANDER. You know what? It seems to me the most interesting evidence is those of you who actually have to make these decisions.

On indexing. Let's say, Mr. Sickler, that the economy goes down, but the indexing formula says you cannot lower the price of your employees. So I would assume the restaurants, if the economy goes down, are one of the first to feel it. Isn't that right? If the economy gets bad——

Mr. SICKLER. Absolutely.

Senator ALEXANDER [continuing]. The restaurant business gets a little worse.

Mr. SICKLER. That is where the family would spend their extra money.

Senator ALEXANDER. So if you cannot lower the cost of your people you hired, then where do you cut? What do you do?

Mr. SICKLER. You try to cut hours. You would like to raise prices, but our prices are high enough right now. It is hard for us to raise the prices of what we sell any higher. We will drive away the rest of the folks that come to our counters at that point.

Senator ALEXANDER. Mr. Rutigliano, what would you cut if the restaurant business went down? The economy goes down, the rest of business goes down, but prices, the indexing keeps going up for employees, what do you cut?

Mr. RUTIGLIANO. Well, you reduce employees and you reduce hours. The main thing people need to remember when it comes to the restaurant business is nobody has to come to us. We are in the discretionary income business. So when the economy downturns, we are usually one of the first things that go.

Senator ALEXANDER. You are talking about a learning job. If the entry level job pays $10, if somebody shows up without any experience, somebody 19, 20 years old and wants a job for $10 an hour, what would you do?

Mr. RUTIGLIANO. For that amount of wage, I would expect some sort of skill set to come along with it. The higher the price, the more experience they would need.

Senator ALEXANDER. What is your experience in terms of entry level, minimum wage employees? How soon do they get a pay increase?

Mr. RUTIGLIANO. In my company? As fast as they demonstrate the ability to do the job, we bump them up right away.

Senator ALEXANDER. And what is the best job training? Is it for them, for your kind of business, to go to the community college or to some other place, or is it better for you just to train them yourselves?

Mr. RUTIGLIANO. We train them ourselves.

Senator ALEXANDER. So for that group is——

Mr. RUTIGLIANO. In fact, the best for our people is to start off in a lower position in the restaurant, show an interest in the hospitality industry, and then move up in our company, and then we hope they stay, and we compensate them accordingly.

Senator ALEXANDER. Would you agree that at a time when we have 12 million unemployed people and a number of them are trying to get on the economic ladder, that if we saw off the bottom rung of it, it will make it harder for them to get a learning job or a chance to move up the ladder?

Mr. RUTIGLIANO. Absolutely. I mean, it is really, truthfully, one of the best things we could do for our young people is to get them into a work environment where they learn how to conduct themselves in a job, punch in, punch out, show up on time, learn some basic job skills.

Senator ALEXANDER. Thank you, Mr. Chairman.

The CHAIRMAN. Thank you, Senator Alexander.

Senator Warren.

Senator WARREN. All right. Thank you very much. Thank you, Mr. Chairman. Thank you, Ranking Member for holding this hearing.

I was very intrigued by the chairman's chart earlier about productivity. And it shows, as I read those numbers and the numbers that you cited, Mr. Dube, that if we just started in 1960—not the high water mark for minimum wage, but a good time on minimum wage—if we started in 1960, and we said that as productivity goes up, that is as workers are producing more, then the minimum wage is going to go up the same. And if that were the case, the minimum wage today would be about $22 an hour.

So my question, Mr. Dube, with the minimum wage at $7.25 an hour, is what happened to the other $14.75? It sure did not go to the worker.

Mr. DUBE. Thanks for the question.

That is correct. Since the early 1970s, what we have seen is a divergence in the prosperities of different sections of our population. For instance, had the minimum wage kept pace with productivity since 1960, you are correct, it would have stood around $22 an hour today.

Now, the answer to your question, who got the other $14? We can answer——

Senator WARREN. And 75 cents.

Mr. DUBE [continuing]. We can answer with the following comparison.

Had the minimum wage grown at the same pace of incomes going to the top 1 percent of the taxpayers, the minimum wage would have stood at $33 an hour before the recession in 2007. What we have seen is really large growth in inequality in this country. And the minimum wage, by the way, in part, has contributed to that.

The academic evidence on this suggests that the gap between the middle and the bottom of the labor market, for instance, about at least half of that gap has been caused by falling minimum wage, and especially so for women workers who tend to be lower paid and more likely to be minimum wage.

Senator WARREN. Dr. Dube, let's just focus on some of those studies. I appreciate that we have two people here who own their own restaurants, and restaurant chains, and I am glad you are here, and I appreciate your being here. But I just want to make sure that I understand the data that you have put together.

The studies you have done, the county-county matches, they look at—and just an estimate on your part—how many different employers; thousands, tens of thousands?

Mr. DUBE. Tens of thousands.

Senator WARREN. Tens of thousands of employers. And is it speculation on what they say they will do?

Mr. DUBE. No, it is actually looking at what happened to employment. It is difficult for us to project what would happen to our business, not if I change something by myself and the rest of the economy was at stasis, but rather, the whole labor market had to pay a higher wage.

This is the difference between, I think, what economists have studied—to look at what happens. How are prices adjusting when not just a single business has to pay a higher wage, but all businesses do. Right? And I think there we find the evidence that there are some price increases. There are no employment losses to be seen for the kind of changes we have looked at.

Senator WARREN. OK. So despite the speculation, what the numbers show in terms of what employers actually did is that we are not seeing job losses.

If I could just ask you, Dr. Dube, because lots of people intuitively think, "If the price goes up, if we raise the minimum wage, then we are going to get fired." Can you just quickly—I read your paper in detail, but if you don't mind—could you just give a quick summary of the reasons that we don't see those layoffs?

Mr. DUBE. Sure. One of the things to keep in mind is that the restaurant industry has an incredibly high turnover.

For instance, today there are millions of people who have left their jobs. At the same time, there are millions of people who are being hired. There are also vacancies. So although there are unemployed restaurant workers, there are also vacant jobs.

This turning happens because, in part, the restaurant industry is a fairly low wage industry and people are taking a higher paid job when they can. What a minimum wage does is it makes it more attractive for workers to stick around. It makes it easier for restaurants to fill vacancies.

What ends up happening, in part, is that a minimum wage increase reduces turnover, and by doing so, kills vacancies and not jobs. And this is something that is important to keep in mind in terms of how a higher wage standard can stabilize these jobs, and actually reduce turnover and recruitment costs.

Senator WARREN. Or if I could say that another way, a sustainable wage actually reduces the cost for the employers, and keeps people employed, and that may be the reason that we are just not seeing job losses when we see an increase in the minimum wage. Is that a fair summary?

Mr. DUBE. That is a much more eloquent summary.

Senator WARREN. You are much too kind. I just wanted to be sure.

And I wanted to ask a question, Mr. Sickler. I appreciate you being here from the National Restaurant Association. I tried to go back and look at the National Restaurant Association's views on minimum wage. Has there ever been a time that the National Restaurant Association supported an increase in the minimum wage?

Mr. SICKLER. I am not sure, quite honestly. I can do some research and get back to you on that. I just don't know. I just don't have that answer.

Senator WARREN. I would appreciate it, because what I think we keep hearing from the Restaurant Association is that if the minimum wage goes up, that jobs will go down. Am I out of time, Mr. Chairman? I apologize.

The CHAIRMAN. All right.

Senator WARREN. I hope we get back to this. Could I say one thing really quickly?

The CHAIRMAN. We will have another round.

Senator WARREN. Fair enough. I apologize, Mr. Chairman.

The CHAIRMAN. We will have another round.

Senator WARREN. Thank you.

The CHAIRMAN. I am going to have to excuse myself. I have an amendment pending on the floor. I will ask Senator Alexander if you would run this for a while?

Senator ALEXANDER. Sure.

The CHAIRMAN. The amendment starts at 11:25. I have to speak on my amendment.

Senator ALEXANDER. Sure.

The CHAIRMAN. Then I will come back and relieve you. Is that OK?

Senator ALEXANDER. I will be here.

The CHAIRMAN. OK. I am going to have to excuse myself. I am going to turn it over to Senator Alexander, and then he can do his 5 minutes, and then get back to you, and then I will be back probably about 11:30 or shortly after 11:30.

Mr. RUTIGLIANO. Can I respond to your comment?

The CHAIRMAN. Sure. Absolutely, absolutely. Please, give a response.

Mr. RUTIGLIANO. I can't imagine any business advocating for increased costs. I mean, it is slightly unreasonable.

Senator WARREN. I am sure. Is it Mr. Prince?

Mr. RUTIGLIANO. No, I am talking about an association. What he does on his own personal level is his business. I pay a lot of people above the minimum wage also, but I am talking about expecting the National Restaurant Association, I think is, you know what I mean.

Senator ALEXANDER. We will have a chance. I will take 5 minutes, and then we will go back to Senator Warren for 5 minutes, and we will have a chance to continue that.

Dr. Dube, you said that if productivity were allowed to determine the minimum wage, it might be $20 or even $33; as much as $33.

I note that the noted conservative economist and columnist Paul Krugman recently wrote that most economists would, ''Agree that setting a minimum wage of, say, $20 an hour would create a lot of problems.''

Do you agree with that?

Mr. DUBE. I do. I do and——

Senator ALEXANDER. And so should we, if we index the minimum wage, should we put a cap on it, sunset it at, say, $20, or $15, or $33?

Mr. DUBE. I think the challenge for the minimum wage has not been high inflation rate, but rather, a stagnating nominal minimum wage.

Senator ALEXANDER. But should we put——

Mr. DUBE. I think that——

Senator ALEXANDER [continuing]. Should it have a cap on it or should it just be allowed to go up as high as it will?

Mr. DUBE. I think for a range of inflation rates we have seen in the last several generations, there would be at no point in time a minimum wage indexed that would outpace, substantially outpace, wages so that it would reach $20 an hour. On the contrary, it wouldn't even rise more than, as I said, maybe $11 an hour at its maximum.

What I want to actually also get back to is your question in terms of setting wages. It is really important to keep in mind that no one is actually advocating for $20 minimum wage that I know of and the reason for that is simple. It is useful to look at the minimum wage in comparison to the median. Historically and for economic and historical reasons, basically around half the median is a very sustainable range. If it goes up to 80 percent, then it's not.

Senator ALEXANDER. But wait a minute, you're saying, you are using those examples as an example of where it might be, where it ought to be. You are suggesting that it could be at that, or might be at that, or too bad it's not at that. That suggests to me that you are.

I have some other questions that I would like to ask. I want to go back to the costs that a small businessperson has to deal with today. I want to focus on the restaurant business. I am not trying to ignore you, Mr. Prince. You've got a very successful business with 23 employees that is a little different than the restaurant business.

The restaurant and hospitality industry is a large employer of low income, and also many minority Americans. Whether a proposal like this would hurt those individuals or help those individuals who work in restaurants, I think, is important.

On the new health care law, the head of a large chain restaurant association told me recently that because of the new health care law and the minimum of $2,000 cost per employee that it would impose on the restaurant that the company would begin, instead of running its store with 90 employees, to try to run it with 70 employees. Does that sound like a familiar strategy to you from restaurant owners you have talked about, either Mr. Sickler or Mr. Rutigliano?

Mr. RUTIGLIANO. It is a familiar strategy. The other one is to increase and decrease hours so that you fall below the——

Senator ALEXANDER. Below the 30 hours.

Mr. RUTIGLIANO [continuing]. What you were going to do. Yes, right.

Senator ALEXANDER. Yes. And the effect of that, though, would be that a number of employees would, because of the increased costs, there would be fewer jobs.

Mr. RUTIGLIANO. Clearly.

Senator ALEXANDER. And you could increase costs a variety of ways in a restaurant, right? One way is to increase the benefit cost. One way is to increase the cost of an entry level wage, correct?

Mr. RUTIGLIANO. Yes, sir.

Senator ALEXANDER. These are costs. In your case, you are saying as a manager and owner of restaurants, 250 employees, will or may, reduce the number of jobs that are available.

Mr. RUTIGLIANO. It would have to reduce the number of jobs. Like I said, we have to remain profitable to my creditors, my family, my employees. I must stay in business. That is why I'm here.

I wanted to address turnover. In the restaurant business, some turnover is expected and it is warranted. A busboy isn't a professional job that somebody is going to have for 30 years. You expect them to move on, either become a waiter or move on to their other job.

A lot of our jobs are with high school and college students that they do this for extra income while they're doing it. And then, after they graduate, they move on. So turnover, some turnover in the restaurant business is expected and warranted.

Senator ALEXANDER. Thank you.

Senator Warren.

Senator WARREN. Thank you very much, Senator Alexander.

I appreciate the point, Mr. Rutigliano, but I want to go back to the question I had earlier. You are telling us what you would do and the National Restaurant Association is telling us, as they have before, what would happen.

Dr. Dube, in the studies of what happens when minimum wages have been raised, and you have done the county to county matches, were restaurants included in the employers in the measurement of whether or not people were laid off?

Mr. DUBE. Restaurants were one of the primary samples that we looked at because of the high incidence of minimum wage workers.

And again, restaurant employment in response to the kind of minimum wage changes, did not respond, on average.

Is it possible that a single employer didn't lay some people off? Is it possible some employer didn't actually expand? That is difficult to say.

The point I am making is on aggregate in the restaurant industry for the kind of minimum wage changes we saw. We did not see employment change noticeably.

Senator WARREN. OK. So the actual behavior of tens of thousands of employers did not reflect a loss in jobs or a decline in jobs when the minimum wage went up. Is that right, Dr. Dube?

Mr. DUBE. That is correct.

Senator WARREN. OK. Thank you.

The question people were asking earlier, and since Senator Alexander went back to it, I would like to go back to it as well, is that when productivity has gone up and profits have gone up, that the minimum wage has, in fact, declined.

So, the question I am asking is not what the right dollar number is here, but really a very different question: when productivity increases, when profits increase, is there a reason that the minimum wage should not increase as well? In other words, that we all should not participate in this increased wealth in our country.

Mr. Prince, would you like to speak to that?

Mr. PRINCE. I completely agree, and I think the thing to remember is we all have more customers than we have employees. So while, his 258 employees will get a raise, his tens and maybe hundreds of thousands of customers will also get a raise, and the sort of the velocity of money in the economy will increase.

We are both in the luxury item business. Nobody needs a record or a CD, but when I look at the 6,000—well, I think so. But when I look at the 6,000 people a week who walk through my door and I think that probably if 10 percent of them—if I hold the Missouri average—make the minimum wage they could have $200 or $300 bucks a month more in their pockets, I know it will be good for my business. And increasing that, would also allow me to hire some people or to try some new things.

Capitalism is all about efficiency and a restaurant employee or a record store employee who is standing there doing nothing because there is no customer walking in because they don't have the money is the least efficient thing in any business.

So increasing the wealth of my customers is a really important thing to me.

Senator WARREN. Thank you. Thank you, Mr. Prince.

Mr. Sickler, I was interested in your point about prices, and yours too, Mr. Rutigliano. During my Senate campaign, I ate a No. 11 at McDonald's many, many times a week, and I know the price on that one: $7.19.

According to the data on the analysis of what would happen if we raised the minimum wage to $10.10 over 3 years, the price increase on that item would be about 4 cents, so instead of being $7.19 it would be $7.23. Are you telling me that is unsustainable?

Mr. SICKLER. Senator Warren, not all restaurants are created equal. I am in the full-service restaurant business. McDonald's has efficiencies and they operate completely differently than I do.

I have many jobs, many jobs that pay well above the minimum wage. We have a retirement plan. We offer health insurance to our salaried employees. So my business is a little different. I can't raise a 4-cent price. I don't operate like a fast food restaurant. So I would hope that you'd at least appreciate the distinction.

Senator WARREN. I do appreciate the distinction and I am not going to be in the business of being a McDonald's representative, but I think they would talk about also having some higher paid jobs and some opportunities for management and advancement as well.

But I get your point. Maybe it is only 4 cents on $7.19, but if your entrees are $14.40, we'll see how fast I can do the math. Are you telling me you can't raise your prices by 8 cents?

Mr. SICKLER. Typically when costs rise, we don't actually raise it just 4 cents. We might actually go a little higher. It has an inflationary effect on the economy. So you may actually be taking away the money you just gave that employee through the minimum wage increase and raise prices throughout the economy.

Senator WARREN. I have to say, you have now switched your argument from what it was going to do to your business, to what it is going to do to the economy.

And I think, Dr. Dube, you have looked at the inflationary effects of increasing the minimum wage. Can you just give us a quick summary on those data?

Mr. DUBE. I think it is uncontroversial amongst economists that a minimum wage increase of this sort would not have a noticeable impact on the overall price level because it's just, the math doesn't add up. The number of people who are getting the raises is not enough for it to show up in some kind of a wage-price spiral.

So the effects on overall price level, very small.

Senator WARREN. Thank you very much. I see my time is up. Thank you, Senator Alexander.

Senator ALEXANDER. Thank you, Senator Warren.

I want to say this respectfully. When we were debating the health care law a couple of years ago, I suggested to my colleagues who were for it, I was concerned about the Medicaid, the imposition of Medicaid costs on States, and they were less concerned about that. And I suggested that anybody who voted for the law ought to be sentenced to go serve as Governor and actually try to administer it for a few years.

And I am intrigued here, listening to a very fine professional academic study of the restaurant—that includes the restaurant business and thinking that maybe everybody who studies it ought to have to run one because there seems to be such a difference of opinion here.

I mean, they are telling you that it is good. That increasing your labor costs is good for business, right? And that is what I am hearing that increasing labor costs by 39 percent will help you have a better business because more people will walk-in the door and buy more food.

I wonder, Mr. Prince, I agree that if people have more money and walk-in to buy more records. But what if the restaurant companies hire 70 people per store instead of 90 people per store, and fewer people can walk in the door? Those who do may have more money, but you might have fewer people.

Mr. PRINCE. First of all, I think the 39 percent number is speculative and specious, that you don't always raise the people above your minimum.

Senator ALEXANDER. That is the amount of the increase in the minimum wage.

Mr. PRINCE. No, what he is saying is he would have to raise everyone in his organization that percent to keep them even, and that's not really how you run a business.

The way we run our business is there are tiered wages and——

Senator ALEXANDER. That is the way he runs his business, I think.

Mr. PRINCE [continuing]. People earn their way up to them.

Senator ALEXANDER. But you're saying that's not the way he runs his business?

Mr. PRINCE. What he is saying is he would have to raise—the statement says he would have to raise everyone's wages that same $2.85.

Senator ALEXANDER. Well, if you said something about how you run your business, I would respect that. Do you not believe he is telling the truth?

Mr. PRINCE. No, no. I'm just saying it is not a necessity and——

Senator ALEXANDER. How do you know it's not? You're not in the restaurant business.

Mr. PRINCE. You're right, I'm not. But I am in the capitalist business.

Senator ALEXANDER. Yes.

Mr. PRINCE. And the way capitalism works is wages should be set based on productivity and their value to the business, and not in relation to one another necessarily.

But the other point you made I thought is much more to the point where you were talking about Medicare costs.

Senator ALEXANDER. Yes.

Mr. PRINCE. This is the thing that sticks in my craw the worst is that I am paying taxes to subsidize my competitors' huge unwillingness to pay realistically high wages.

I just got this from the State of Missouri last week. In Missouri, the Missouri HealthNet, which is our Medicaid system——

Senator ALEXANDER. Because you're paying higher wages, you resent that somebody else pays lower wages.

Mr. PRINCE. Because I'm subsidizing those lower wages.

Senator ALEXANDER. But I thought you were paying higher wages because it created more loyal employees, less turnover, and because it was better for the community.

Mr. PRINCE. Yes, what I'm saying though, is I resent the fact that part of the taxes I pay go to subsidize my competition. The numbers are staggering.

McDonald's $3.7 million a quarter in Missouri Medicaid is paid to McDonald's employees; 6.5 million—Casey's, Dollar General, Sonic Restaurants, $1.5 million a quarter; Wendy's, Subway, Taco Bell $1 million a quarter. That's $18 million dollars a quarter to a not particularly wealthy State like Missouri to just the top eight corporations, all of which are hugely profitable corporations.

The minimum wage argument is about the relationship between the bottom wage and corporate profits, the bottom wage and the top wage. It seems to me that you guys make the rules. You guys set the ground rules under which businesses need to compete and then our job is to be efficient in competing in them.

Senator ALEXANDER. But listen——

Mr. PRINCE. And if you set fair rules for workers, then we learn to be more efficient to compete.

Senator ALEXANDER [continuing]. There's another rule-setter that some of us subscribe to called the market.

Mr. PRICE. Yes.

Senator ALEXANDER. And the market can set the rules. Now, a record store is going to be different than a restaurant.

What would you say to what you just heard, Mr. Rutigliano?

Mr. RUTIGLIANO. About price—well, it is essentially, he is setting price controls. It is no different than setting price controls. You are doing that with wages. Does that make sense?

Senator ALEXANDER. It does to me.

Mr. RUTIGLIANO. Like you would never tell somebody what to sell something for.

Mr. PRINCE. I'm actually talking—how can I put this?

Mr. RUTIGLIANO. It's not really a free economy.

Mr. PRINCE. That's not the case. In fact, I deal in an item that has been commodified and the price has gone down by 30 percent in the last 10 years. These are the things in our system that you have to address to, that you have to create efficiencies to make up for.

Senator ALEXANDER. This is a tremendous——

Mr. PRINCE. The other thing, just so you know, is reach, and I'm not talking about just record stores here. I work on a street that has 35 independently owned retail establishments. I am talking about retail. I don't know the restaurant business, but I know a whole lot about retail, and in retail the prices are set by the market, by what the market will pay. It is why a beer is $10 bucks in Yankee Stadium and $2 bucks across the street in Murray's Bar.

Senator ALEXANDER. And wages are generally set by what the market will pay as well.

Mr. PRINCE. Except that you set the floor.

Senator ALEXANDER. Senator Harkin—I beg your pardon?

Mr. PRINCE. I'm sorry. I don't mean to interrupt, but you guys set the floor and——

Senator ALEXANDER. Not if I was doing it. I would let the market do it.

Mr. PRINCE. But I think——

Senator ALEXANDER. I am for a maximum wage, not a minimum wage and my time is up. I have been informed by Senator Harkin that he won't be coming back, and we have to go vote. I want to personally thank the six witnesses. All of you have gone to a considerable effort, one coming all the way from Georgia, I think, if that's right.

Ms. FLEURIO. Yes.

Senator ALEXANDER. Two have driven down from your businesses. All six of you, thank you very much for a very spirited, informative hearing. We thank you for your written comments.

If you have any additional comments that you would like to make, we would like to have those within 10 days.

I will ask Senator Warren if she has any other comment before we conclude, and then we will adjourn the hearing, and we will go vote.

Senator WARREN. No, thank you very much, Ranking Member. Appreciate it.

Senator ALEXANDER. OK, Senator Warren. Thank you for coming. And thanks to all of you for being here.

[Additional material follows.]

ADDITIONAL MATERIAL

NATIONAL RESTAURANT ASSOCIATION,
WASHINGTON, DC 20036,
March 28, 2013.

Hon. TOM HARKIN, *Chairman,*
Committee on Health, Education, Labor, and Pensions,
U.S. Senate,
Washington, DC 20510.

Hon. LAMAR ALEXANDER, *Ranking Member,*
Committee on Health, Education, Labor, and Pensions,
U.S. Senate,
Washington, DC 20510.

Re: Hearing on ''Keeping up with a Changing Economy: Indexing the Minimum Wage''

DEAR CHAIRMAN HARKIN AND RANKING MEMBER ALEXANDER: Thank you for the opportunity to testify on behalf of the National Restaurant Association at the March 14, 2013, hearing, ''Keeping up with a Changing Economy: Indexing the Minimum Wage.'' I appreciated the opportunity to discuss with the committee the negative impact that an increase in the minimum wage would have on small business owners like me.

I would like to expand and reply, for the record, about two statements made at the hearing. Specifically, it was erroneously stated that raising the minimum wage would have no impact on those individuals earning above minimum wage. Second, it was suggested that the minimum wage should be at $22, ''to keep pace with worker productivity since 1960,'' or even $33, to keep pace with ''the top 1 percent of income earners.''

As to the first point, it is true that I do not absolutely have to raise the wages of my higher paid employees, if the minimum wage forces me to pay entry-level workers more. However, if I do not, at the very least, the difference between the entry-level wage and the wage for those who have earned merit increases would shrink. But, deciding to raise or not raise the wages of higher paid employees is not simply a matter of efficiency, as it was characterized.

Employees understand fairness, and that is why I award merit increases. To reduce the value of those merit increases by requiring me to raise my entry-level wage without raising the wage of other employees would limit the amount of opportunities for employees to learn the value of a job well-done, and be rewarded for it appropriately.

Furthermore, the difference between the minimum wage—a rate of pay at which very few of my crew members remain for very long—and the top rate of pay is not great, when compared with the wide range of salaries in the corporate world. This fact augments the pressure to increase all wages when the entry-level wage goes up. Reducing the difference between the entry-level wage and the pay of higher earners does much more to devalue my existing employees' efforts than it does to help those whose wages would rise. Entry-level workers taking their first step in the process of learning how to succeed in the workplace can quickly prove and earn their worth.

Thus, assuming that the impact and cost to an employer of raising the minimum wage can be calculated by looking only at those currently making the minimum wage is simply being detached from reality.

The second statement, regarding the idea of coupling minimum wage increases to either the increase in the average productivity of American workers since 1960 or to increases in earnings of the top 1 percent of taxpayers, ignores the realities of different industries and sectors of the economy. A Senator even asked ''What happened to the other $14.75? It sure did not go to the worker!,'' when referring to the difference between the current Federal minimum wage ($7.25) and what she thought it should be ($22), if it kept up with productivity since 1960.

It is extremely dangerous for policymakers to formulate such broad extrapolations in a diverse economy such as ours. For example, Google's profit-per-employee in 2011 was $336,000, while the average chain restaurant's profit-per-employee was less than $5,000. Thus, while an increase in the hourly rate of $14.75 for a full-time employee of Google would be barely noticeable, the same increase for an average chain restaurant worker would turn a profit-per-employee into a deficit-per-employee.

In other words, in the case of your average chain restaurant, such an increase would turn a profitable business into a non-viable one. I was shocked to see how even the rate of a minimum wage increase to $33 an hour was so carelessly thrown around by proponents of a minimum wage increase.

If I learned anything from participating in this hearing, it is the danger of indexing the minimum wage, particularly if doing so back in 1960 would have led us to a minimum wage of $22 or $33 today. Most people want to make more money, but the market dictates the prices of my products and how much I can pay my workers, my suppliers, my landlords, and others, while still making a profit.

I thank you again for the opportunity to testify on behalf of the National Restaurant Association. I respectfully ask that this letter be included in the hearing record.

Regards,

MEL SICKLER.

———

RESPONSE TO QUESTIONS OF SENATOR ALEXANDER BY BRAD AVAKIAN

Thank you for the questions and opportunity to discuss Oregon's successful experience indexing our State's minimum wage to inflation. Below, please find the Oregon Bureau of Labor and Industries responses to the committee's questions.

In your testimony, you claimed of Oregon's experience that "every dime in the increase of the minimum wage is a dime that gets reinvested back into community businesses," and that "small businesses in fact are dependent on that kind of a local purchasing power." A recent study by Economist Joseph Sabia found that in lower skilled industries sensitive to minimum wage increases—including retail, food service, and accommodations—each 10 percent increase in the State minimum wage is associated with a 2 to 4 percent decline in State GDP generated by these lower skilled industries. Economist and former Chair of President Obama's Council of Economic Advisers Christina Romer, writing in *The New York Times*, likewise concluded that any increase in consumer spending and consequent output growth resulting from a minimum wage increase would be negligible in the context of a $15 trillion economy.

Question 1. Do you disagree with the conclusions of these distinguished economists? What objective economic data prove your claim that "every dime" of increased minimum wages in Oregon has been spent in local businesses? What objective economic data prove the dependence of Oregon's small businesses on indexed annual minimum wage increases?

Answer 1. Consumer spending makes up 70 percent of our country's total economy, which is why stagnant wages limit growth and contribute to a weak economy.

One must be careful to not compare the effect local consumer spending has on local businesses with its relation to the Nation's entire $15 trillion economy, which includes exports, investments, securities and other intangible goods. Minimum wage earners do not generally participate in those markets.

The Federal minimum wage—and that of every State—is below the Federal poverty threshold, with minimum wage earners spending the vast majority of their money on the essentials of life such as housing, food, gas or public transportation. It is, therefore, the local businesses that are affected by the purchasing power of minimum wage earners.

As an example, Oregon's modest 2013 minimum wage increase of 15 cents per hour will affect about 127,000 workers. The increase equates to about $23 million in new money to minimum wage workers, who in turn spend that money on goods and household essentials. This modest 15 cent adjustment meant that the average directly affected worker will have over $400 more this year to pay for the increased costs of basic necessities like food and gas. Without the wage increase, it's a fair conclusion that $23 million would not have gone to workers trying to keep pace with the rising cost of everyday goods.

A recent study by the Center for Economic and Policy Research "Why Does the Minimum Wage Have No Discernible Effect on Employment?" also noted the disparity in savings rates between high-wage and low-wage workers:

> Particularly when the economy is in a recession or operating below full employment, a minimum-wage increase may also increase demand for firms' goods and services, offsetting the increase in employer costs.

> Since the minimum wage transfers income from employers (who generally have a high savings rate) to low-wage workers (who generally have a low savings rate), a minimum-wage rise could spur consumer spending. This increase in spending could potentially compensate firms for the direct increase in wage costs.

Question 2. In claiming that businesses depend on the purchasing power of minimum-wage earners, you argued that annual inflationary adjustments like those in Oregon were necessary to sustain businesses. But the minimum wage has built into it a natural inflationary adjustment based on demand. Since 2010, the number of hourly workers earning the minimum wage in this country has decreased by more than 18 percent. So, isn't the positive effect you have described already going on?

Answer 2. Oregon does not construe a minimum wage to have a "natural inflationary adjustment based on demand." In fact, a corporation looking to increase shareholder profits might decide to stagnate or decrease wages to achieve a greater profit margin. During a down economy, the risk increases with greater competition for customers and dollars.

Attaching the minimum wage to the Consumer Price Index so that it increases with inflation guarantees that wages will keep pace with the rising cost of goods and services. In addition, an indexed minimum wage also provides a steady, predictable system businesses can count on for projected labor costs. The result is reliable purchasing power for our lowest wage earners.

Question 3. You testified that Oregon law guarantees a minimum wage to wait staff, and that Oregon's restaurant industry is doing well. However, another witness at the hearing testified that after peaking at 16.4 employees per establishment in 1996, the average number of workers in Oregon's restaurants has continually declined to 13.8 in 2011, a 2.6 worker decrease. This job loss began when Oregon's minimum wage began rising above the Federal level in 1997 and has continued. By contrast, on the national level restaurants have maintained a steady level of employment since 1996. If Oregon's restaurant staffing levels had similarly remained unchanged, Oregon's restaurants would employ 23,500 more workers today. As the top State labor official, what proof do you have that these 23,500 lost jobs in Oregon's restaurant industry were not related to Oregon's ever-increasing minimum wage?

Answer 3. Oregon guarantees a minimum wage to restaurant workers out of a sense of basic fairness and belief that servers are not overpaid. As such, our State has no plans to impose a "tip credit" on wait staff or otherwise rollback Oregon's voter-approved minimum wage.

Under Oregon's successful minimum wage model, the National Restaurant Association still projects that the number of Oregon restaurant employees will increase 12 percent over the next 10 years (Source: National Restaurant Association Fact Sheet, *Oregon Restaurant Industry At a Glance*). Notably, the increase is higher than the 9.1 percent projected for the Nation as whole, as compiled by the National Restaurant Association's State-by-State fact sheets:

State	Current employees	2023 Projections, NRA
AL	167,200	190,700
AK	27,700	31,600
AZ	262,200	303,800
AR	114,200	130,000
CA	1,475,100	1,615,600
CO	239,400	272,000
CT	144,200	151,400
DE	44,100	50,200
DC	52,800	56,100
FL	844,800	968,500
GA	378,200	431,300
HI	85,100	89,400
ID	57,800	64,000
IL	517,900	553,400
IN	296,100	319,000
IA	140,300	151,000
KS	125,900	137,300
KT	191,300	207,900
LA	197,300	210,800
ME	58,700	63,400
MD	232,700	249,000
MA	313,500	331,700
MI	390,900	414,700

State	Current employees	2023 Projections, NRA
MN	246,300	262,800
MS	109,000	120,300
MO	275,100	294,400
MT	49,700	52,800
NE	88,500	94,400
NV	192,100	220,600
NH	60,900	65,700
NJ	318,200	337,800
NM	83,400	93,800
NY	750,900	801,500
NC	411,800	467,400
ND	39,500	45,300
OH	526,700	558,600
OK	151,200	167,400
OR	**171,900**	**192,600**
PA	535,000	561,700
RI	49,600	52,800
SC	196,600	220,300
SD	43,400	47,600
TN	267,600	290,800
TX	1,074,200	1,245,000
UT	103,300	117,700
VT	24,700	26,400
VA	348,100	383,600
WA	280,200	310,200
WV	74,200	78,000
WI	254,100	269,500
WY	26,400	28,200
Total	**13,110,000**	**14,400,000**

If paying Oregon wait staff a fair minimum wage were a determinative factor in employment levels, Oregon restaurant employment levels would not be projected to rise higher than national averages.

According to the National Restaurant Association, restaurants remain ''a driving force in Oregon's economy.'' In fact, Oregon has 8,867 restaurants, with total employment in the restaurant sector at 10-percent of our State's workforce.

Question 4. At the hearing, you claimed in response to the previous data that the job losses Oregon experienced were due to the State's dependence on the timber, agriculture, and technology industries and the sensitivity of those sectors to the recent recession. But job losses in the timber, agriculture, and technology industries do not explain the specific job losses in the restaurant industry. The recession also would not explain the gradual decline in restaurant employment dating back to 1996, well before the recent recession began. What evidence do you have that job losses in the timber, agriculture, and technology sectors during recessions cause job losses in Oregon's restaurant industry even in those years when the economy is performing well?

Answer 4. I do not assert that job losses in timber, agriculture, and technology sectors cause job losses in Oregon's restaurant industry. Although, it stands to reason that as more families become unemployed in various industry sectors, their corresponding decreased purchasing power could lead to many fewer restaurant meals and, therefore, less revenue to sustain jobs within restaurants.

It's worth noting that at 172,000 employees, Oregon's restaurant sector represents 10 percent of the State's workforce, exactly on par with the national average. As noted above, our healthy restaurant industry—despite paying its workers a fair wage—will see employment numbers increase more than the national average over the next decade, according to the National Restaurant Association's projections.

RESPONSE TO QUESTIONS OF SENATOR HARKIN AND SENATOR ALEXANDER
BY ARINDRAJIT DUBE, PH.D.

SENATOR HARKIN

Question 1. In your testimony, you talked about the inefficiency of the current practice of long periods of stagnation in the minimum wage, followed by sharp increases. Could you please expand on this? What are the inefficiencies? Why would indexing the wage to inflation be more efficient?

Answer 1. The nominal Federal minimum wage remained stagnant for 9 years between 1981 and 1990, and for 10 years between 1997 and 2007. The real minimum wage declined during these episodes due to inflation, and these decreases were followed by sharp increases in the nominal and real minimum wage. These adjustments were largely based on political factors, not economic ones. Similarly, State-level increases in the minimum wage during these periods of Federal inaction were based more on political rather than economic considerations.

These large swings and variations in minimum wages—both over time and across areas—create uncertainties for both businesses and families with low-wage workers, and may adversely affect their spending and investment decisions. Having a predictable increase in the minimum wage from an automatic process would aid families and businesses plan for the changes and would mitigate any short-term disruptions such as liquidity shortfalls, and would make it easier for consumers to absorb any (small) price increases.

For these and other reasons, whatever the *level* of the real minimum wage may be, using indexation to ensure future *changes* occur regularly and in small increments makes economic sense. For this reason, even some minimum wage skeptics such as the economist Daniel Hammermesh support indexation.

Question 2. Some people are concerned that indexing would mean that wages would increase even during times of high unemployment. Did your research look at periods of high unemployment? What did it find regarding the effects of minimum wage increases on employment during those times?

Answer 2. Our research has investigated whether employment of highly affected groups (like teens) responds to minimum wages differently when the overall unemployment rate is high. We did not find any evidence that teen employment was negatively affected by minimum wage increases, including during episodes with higher overall unemployment. For the range of minimum wage increases we have seen over the past few decades, our research suggests that effects on employment are small in magnitude—under both relatively soft and relatively strong labor market conditions.

Question 3. I find it very interesting that your work shows that raising the minimum wage can reduce the poverty rate. Could you please expand on this? Do you expect that indexing the minimum wage will maintain poverty reductions into the future?

Answer 3. In my new research, I find that a 10 percent increase in minimum wages would reduce poverty by around 3 percent. This suggests that the proposed increase in minimum wage under Harkin-Miller would reduce the official poverty rate from by around 1.8 percentage points, from 15.1 percent to 13.3 percent—a moderate-sized reduction that would mostly reverse the increases in poverty we have seen since the onset of the 2007 recession. These estimates are similar to evidence present in research conducted by David Neumark and William Wascher (2011). Although they do not directly report it, their evidence also indicates that a 10 percent increase in minimum wages would reduce poverty by around 3 percent for the widest group they studied (18–44-year-old adults and family heads).

A reasonably high minimum wage can be a part of an anti-poverty policy portfolio, and boosts the efficacy of other policies such as the Earned Income Tax Credit. But we should also keep in mind that effects of minimum wages are likely to be moderate in size, since many families under the poverty level lack any substantial attachment to the labor force. Around half of the working age adults in poverty do not work. As a consequence, we should not expect the minimum wage to solve the problem of poverty by itself. By the same token, just because minimum wage increases do not aid poor families lacking ties to the labor market should not detract from the ability of the policy to aid low-income families as a whole.

Question 4. If the minimum wage had been indexed to inflation since 1968, what would the economy look like today? How would the economic factors that you discuss in your testimony be different?

Answer 4. Had the minimum wage been indexed to inflation since 1968, it would stand at $10.60/hour today. The economy would not be radically altered, but there would be some important differences. An economy with a $10.60/hour minimum wage would be somewhat less unequal when it came to wages and family incomes. A minimum wage worker would make a little more than half the wage earned by the median U.S. worker. The greater purchasing power for low-income families would mean that poverty rates would be somewhat lower than they are today, maybe by around 2 percentage points. Low-wage workers would tend to stick around in their jobs a little longer—so labor turnover would be around 10 percent lower at those jobs. The overall number low-wage jobs would not likely be very different.

Finally, I would not expect any noticeable difference in macro economic conditions such as the unemployment or inflation rates.

Question 5. In your testimony, you noted that the minimum wage would be at $22 per hour if it had kept up with productivity growth, or at $33 per hour if it had kept up with the growth in income of the top 1 percent of earners. Please clarify if you believe that the minimum wage should be at those levels today, or if you foresee the minimum wage, if indexed, ever reaching those levels (in real terms)?

Answer 5. It is useful to compare how the earnings of minimum wage workers have fared against a host of benchmarks, such as the cost of living, the median wage, average productivity, as well as incomes of top earners. They show the magnitude of absolute and relative income losses of low-wage earners. This is why I provided these comparisons in my testimony.

As I also explicitly stated in my written testimony,

" ... [t]his evidence does not suggest that the minimum wage should be increased to $22 or $24 per hour. Rather, the exercise demonstrates how different the growth rates have been for incomes going to those at the bottom of the labor market as compared to the economy as a whole, and to those at the top end of the distribution. Of course, there are many reasons behind this dramatic rise in inequality, including technological change, falling rates of unionization, deindustrialization, increased trade, deregulation and more. And we certainly cannot expect minimum wages alone to solve the challenge of growing inequality."

I specifically recommended comparing the minimum wage to the median wage for an economically appropriate determination of the statutory minimum—a standard practice among economists.

"A comparison to the median wage also clarifies why [a minimum wage] around $10/hour is reasonable while $20/hour is not. The median wage today is around $20/hour. There are no known cases where the minimum wage was set equal to the median in a capitalist economy. However, there are many cases, including here in the United States, where it was set at or slightly above half the median wage."

To reiterate, I do not think setting a minimum wage of $22/hour would be reasonable. And the minimum wage under the Harkin-Miller would never reach those levels in real terms, as indexation to the CPI would—by definition—keep the real value of minimum wage around $9.38/hour in today's dollars, or $10.10 in current dollars at the time of full phase-in.

SENATOR ALEXANDER

Question 1. Are you aware that fully ⅔ of Americans age 16 or older living below the poverty line do not work at all? Raising the minimum wage does not help these people, and it may hurt by eliminating job opportunities. Do you agree with Christina Romer's statement that "A job may ultimately be the most valuable thing for a family struggling to escape poverty"?

Answer 1. As I stated in my written testimony,

" ... [m]inimum wages tend to increase income going to working class and poor families. However, the anti-poverty aspect of minimum wage is limited by the fact that many families under the poverty line do not have substantial attachment to the labor force."

Around half of working age (16–64) individuals in families earning below the poverty line do not have jobs.

For an issue as multi-faceted as poverty, we cannot expect a single policy tool to fully solve the problem. This is why it is important to enact policies to stimulate spending and jobs, and I agree with Professor Romer on that point. It is also why direct support to families in poverty with programs such as food stamps is critical.

However, it is also true—as Professor Romer herself pointed out—that half of the workers who would be affected by a minimum wage increase are in families making less than $40,000 a year. And many of them are in families earning below the Federal poverty guideline. The best evidence on the topic of minimum wages and family incomes supports the view that increases in minimum wages have a moderate but clear effect on reducing poverty: the proposed increase under Harkin-Miller would be expected to reduce the poverty rate by around 1.8 percentage points. It would also increase the effectiveness of another employment-based poverty-fighting program, the Earned Income Tax Credit—a program that Professor Romer and others have proposed expanding.

An effective solution to the problem of poverty requires a portfolio of policies. A reasonably high minimum wage would be a valuable, though limited, part of that portfolio.

Question 2. American ingenuity has created a tremendous surge in productivity per employee over the last several decades. New technologies and robotic technology have made employees so much more productive, that in many industries fewer of them are needed. Industrial robot sales increased 38 percent between 2010 and 2012, and are expected to set a new record this year. Are you concerned that raising the cost of low-skilled labor at a time when the need for it is diminishing will eliminate these jobs even faster and hurt the very people we are trying to help?

Answer 2. Labor saving technical change, including the adoption of robotic technology, is an ongoing process that has reduced the demand for routinized labor. As work by MIT economist David Autor has documented, these changes have reduced demand for middle-skill jobs while actually *boosting* employment growth in low-skill service work (along with increasing higher skill jobs requiring cognitive and analytical skills). This view is widely shared among economists.

These growing low-skill service jobs—short order cooks, bussers, janitors, home health aides—involve non-routine manual tasks. In other words, they are less susceptible to replacement by either robots or offshore workers, which is precisely why they have grown over the past several decades. An increasing number of workers are performing these jobs, which tend to pay low wages. Many of these workers are earning at or slightly above the statutory minimum wage. Boosting the pay level for these low-wage service jobs is actually a fairly effective way of helping low-skill workers, given the relatively limited possibilities for substituting such workers with technology or offshore labor in the near future.

Question 3. You acknowledge in your testimony that upward adjustments of the minimum wage will result in consumer price increases, particularly in "high impact sectors like restaurants." Christina Romer and other economists have concluded that the price increases in some of these businesses, like fast food and discount retailers, fall heaviest on consumers with very low incomes, those who an increased minimum wage is intended to help. Are you concerned about increasing the cost of living for Americans who may live on fixed income and or have no income because they cannot find work?

Answer 3. Because a minimum wage increase will substantially boost pay for low-wage workers and their families, the net gain to low-income families from the proposed policy outweighs the small price increases that would likely occur.

For example, a family earning an income right around the Federal poverty guideline can expect their nominal incomes to rise by around 10 percent from the proposed policy. The overall price increase from the proposed policy would be less than 0.5 percent. So in net, low-income families are likely to be substantially better off from the policy than without it, even factoring in the small price increases.

RESPONSE TO QUESTIONS OF SENATOR ALEXANDER BY LEW PRINCE

Question 1. I saw you quoted in a news article saying you closed one store because the economy was poor in that location and you could no longer make a profit. One element of the Chairman's bill would disallow minimum wage *decreases* when the Consumer Price Index decreases, as it did in 2009, as protection of workers in tough economic times. But employers such as you also have to deal with the challenges of a bad economy, which can be even worse is specific depressed areas. Are you concerned that artificially elevated labor costs in the face of deflation could force more struggling businesses to close when the economy gets tough, which will eliminate more jobs?

Answer 1. No. I think this is an academic question as the CPI almost never goes down.

The point of indexing is to help business owners plan wage increases into our annual budgeting process. Indexing would have kept businesses out of the "shock" raise situation we're now in if we'd had it since the 1960s. Here in Missouri where we've had indexing since 2006. I haven't run into one business owner or news story stating that the slow, incremental change has had any significant effect on their profits.

Also, higher minimum wages aren't "artificially high." Ideally wages would reflect a societal value that a person working 40 hours should be able to support a family on a paycheck. The theory I work on is that your job in the Congress is to set the rules (wages, safety net, child labor, working conditions) based on our national values and my job as CEO is to figure out how to make my business work within those rules. What bugs me is when I have to compete with businesses that are playing by different rules because they have special tax breaks because they can afford lobbyists. Or can get away with the current artificially low minimum because the taxpayers pick up the difference of the real cost of living through financing the safety net (food stamps, Medicaid, etc).

In retail we deal with recession by adjusting our product mix to find cheaper items, lowering overhead by negotiating better deals with some of our suppliers (they're more pliable when biz is down) and occasionally cutting back on labor hours. Mostly, we learn to live with less profit. It's just a fact of life. And is usually temporary. *If you think that you can fine tune any capitalist economy to prevent job loss in a recession, you are fooling yourself. The answer to recession is stimulus and the biggest stimulus comes from government spending.*

The specifics of the death of our Granite City store was that a regional store in a steel mill town became unfeasible. In the time we were there (17 years—the first 15 were profitable) the town went from three mills working three shifts to one mill working one shift; the record industry contracted by about 60 percent. and the price of gas more than doubled, so customers driving more than a couple of miles cut their number of annual visits significantly. The city offered us free prime space in the middle of downtown if we'd stay and the outlook for Granite City was so bleak that we declined.

Question 2. In your statement, you stated "My bookkeeper and I have already begun discussions in anticipation of your actions." What did you mean by this? What sort of preparations do you anticipate having to undertake if the minimum wage raises costs?

Answer 2. In a situation like this we can either cut costs or stimulate growth. Our costs are pretty much cut to the bone, and besides, I'm optimistic about the U.S. economy, so Vintage Vinyl chooses stimulus.

We have a projected annual budget and make quarterly adjustments. If my labor costs are going up, we look for ways to make up the cost. Usually this means increasing our potential profit by upping our risk. I run Vintage Vinyl conservatively, so increasing risk would entail Debbie (bookkeeper), John, my head buyer and Leon, my store manager, and I looking at the product mix and seeing where we can create more sales by adding product that we have heretofore forgone as more risky.

We have about 60,000 titles of LP, CD and DVD in the store. They fall into two categories: new and used. The new stuff comes from record and movie companies and the used we buy from individuals, institutions, and estates.

The following simplifies a complicated process . . .

Right now most of the inventory bought brand new from record labels and movie companies is on a 30-day billing cycle. In other words, if I buy something on the first of the month, the bill comes due on the 31st. If I haven't sold it, I have to buy it—with money that comes out of profit—or return it. Our computer tracks "days held," so we usually only reorder items that turned in less than 30 days. That way we maximize our ROI (return on investment) on 30-day merchandise.

To increase profit on these new items by increasing risk, we would dip into our credit line to pay for 31-plus day sellers that past experience says will sell before the interest on the borrowed money eats up the profit. We will work with the staff to choose titles they think we can do effective in-store marketing on.

We also looked at investing more in used LPs, which are sailing out the door right now. They are our highest profit items. So we dipped into the credit line to increase the depth and breadth of our used LP inventory in the hopes of increasing sales. We are buying slightly riskier (that is more specialized—slower selling) titles. We offer sellers a lower price on these and believe the increased markup will cover the cost of the money and that the increased profit will allow us to multiply the effect of the borrowed money when we reinvest some of it in more copies of these titles. We can do this because we have established ourselves as paying the most in the region for used titles.

We project the increased profit from these strategies will allow us to cover getting everyone over $10 per hour by the end of the summer and pay back the borrowed money in time to make it available again for Holiday Season inventory purchases.

We also will spend a little to advertise our broader selection in hopes of increasing traffic.

These kinds of options are open to any creative businessperson. They differ from industry to industry and are not as cut and dried as I put them, but the creative management of risk and reward is the basis of success in a capitalist enterprise.

NATIONAL RESTAURANT ASSOCIATION,
WASHINGTON, DC 20036,
April 9, 2013.

Hon. TOM HARKIN, *Chairman,*
Committee on Health, Education, Labor, and Pensions,
U.S. Senate,
Washington, DC 20510.

Hon. LAMAR ALEXANDER, *Ranking Member,*
Committee on Health, Education, Labor, and Pensions,
U.S. Senate,
Washington, DC 20510.

Re: Followup Questions from Hearing on ''Keeping up with a Changing Economy: Indexing the Minimum Wage''

DEAR CHAIRMAN HARKIN AND RANKING MEMBER ALEXANDER: On behalf of the National Restaurant Association (''the Association''), I thank you, once again, for the opportunity to expand on the facts in order to better educate the committee on the impact the proposed legislation, The Fair Minimum Wage Act of 2013 (S. 460), would have on our industry's businesses. I do encourage you to continue this dialog by contacting the Association's professional labor and workforce staff.

The Association is the preeminent representative of an industry made up of 980,000 restaurant and foodservice outlets employing 13.1 million people—about 10 percent of the American workforce. Despite being an industry of mostly small businesses, the restaurant industry is the Nation's second-largest private-sector employer.

Some of the issues raised in these questions do not apply to my business. In addition, because of the technical nature of the questions and the fact that I am not an expert on the historical positions of the Association, I am relying on the Association's staff to be able to provide the committee with full and detailed answers to some of these questions. Thus, I do encourage you to contact them for more details, which they would be happy to provide.

Question 1. Do you think that small, predictable raises in the minimum wage that happen once a year are easier to plan for than irregular increases every 5 to 10 years?

Answer 1. Revenues are not predictable. The economy is not predictable. Thus, it would be an extreme burden on restaurants, which are very labor-intensive, to have the entry level wage increase arbitrarily, no matter how predictable. The danger of automatic increases became clear during the hearing when it was stated that the minimum wage should be at $22, if it had kept pace with worker productivity since 1960, or even $33, if it had kept pace with the earnings of those in the top 1 percent income bracket.

Question 2. When the minimum wage goes up, does it also affect your competitors? Does a minimum wage increase put you at a competitive disadvantage?

Answer 2. Restaurants do not only compete with other restaurants. The products and the experience our members sell are optional. For example, a family can always choose to eat at home. Thus, raising menu prices and trying to pass the added costs on to their customers is simply not a viable option, particularly in this challenging economic environment, because many customers will just not get their food from restaurants.

As the following chart shows, also presented in my testimony, even a 5 percent increase in menu prices would not be enough to account for the sharp increase in labor costs called for in The Fair Minimum Wage Act of 2013 (S. 460). That assumes that a 5 percent menu price increase would even be possible, which according to the Bureau of Labor Statistics hasn't happened since 1982.

Instead, most restaurants will be forced to reduce their employees' hours, postpone plans for new hiring, and/or reduce the number of employees in their restaurants. Only a small minority of restaurants will be able to handle a 39 percent minimum wage increase without taking actions that will harm workers.

Bottom Line Impact of an Increase in the Federal Minimum Wage to $10.10*

Typical Restaurant With Annual Sales of $900,000

	Before	Public policy impact	After
Income			
Food and Beverage Sales	$900,000	Menu Prices (up) 5%	$945,000
Expenses			
Cost of Food & Beverage Sales	$288,000	Food Costs (up) ??	$288,000
3Salaries, Wages & Benefit	306,000	Labor Costs (up) 22%	374,000
Utility Costs	31,500	Energy Costs (up) ??	31,500
Restaurant Occupancy Costs	63,000		63,000
General/Administrative Expenses	27,000		27,000
Other Expenses	145,000		145,000
Total Expenses	$860,500		$928,500
Pre-Tax Income	$39,500	Pre-Tax Income (down) 58%	$16,500
(Percent of Total Sales)	4.4%		1.7%

Source: National Restaurant Association calculations.

*Also includes an increase in the cash wage for tipped employees to 70 percent of the Federal minimum wage.

Question 3. Has the National Restaurant Association ever in its history supported a minimum wage increase? Does the National Restaurant Association believe that there should be a minimum wage at all?

Answer 3. The staff of the Association went back to look at the last time the Senate seriously considered and passed a minimum wage increase, in 2007, and found that the Association did not oppose passage of that legislation. While the package did not completely mitigate the impact of the minimum wage increase, the Association commended Congress for recognizing the importance of granting small businesses the necessary resources to partially offset the consequences of the minimum wage increase.

The Fair Minimum Wage Act of 2013 (S. 460) contains no mitigating provisions. Thus, the Association will continue to oppose S. 460 in its current form. In these economic times, Congress should not be trying to make it harder for small employers, such as myself, to hire more deserving people. Instead, as I asked in my testimony, Congress should focus on policies that encourage more people, not fewer, to enter the workforce. Our collective goal should be to get our young people hired and on the path to achieving the American Dream.

As to the second part of this question, the Association is not aware of legislation introduced calling for the abolishment of the Federal minimum wage. Once such legislation is introduced, as they did with the minimum wage increase legislation in 2007 and, currently, with S. 460, the Association's staff will analyze such legislation *in toto* and decide then whether to take a position on behalf of the industry.

Question 4. Your testimony states that the median hourly earnings of waiters and waitresses range from $16 for entry-level servers to $22 for more experienced servers after tips. However, data from Bureau of Labor Statistics, which is the gold standard for wage data, shows that in 2011, waiters and waitresses had a median hourly wage of $8.93 after tips. What is the source of your data? Why do the figures in your testimony differ so much from the official data? Please provide a copy of your source data, including detailed methodology.

Answer 4. The National Restaurant Association is a frequent user of BLS data, and its staff agrees that BLS is typically the gold standard when it comes to wage and labor data. However, one shortcoming is the wage data for tipped employees in the Occupational Employment Statistics (OES) survey, which is the source of the $8.93 figure cited in the question above for waiters and waitresses.

Restaurant industry experts strongly believe the reported OES wage data greatly underestimates the actual earnings of waiters and waitresses, when tips are included. The National Restaurant Association is currently working with BLS field economists to rectify this problem, and it would be happy to follow up with the committee when the issue is resolved.

As background, here is a brief summary of the problem. Originally, the OES survey, which is fielded among a nationwide sample of employers, asked respondents to only report the employer-paid wages, and exclude tips. Then, a few years ago, the OES survey began asking employers to include both employer-paid wages and tips in their responses. However, the data has never reflected an uptick in the numbers that would be expected with this change in the survey methodology. Once again, the BLS field economists are aware of this situation, and they are currently working on a solution.

Given the shortcomings in the OES data, the National Restaurant Association has fielded surveys of restaurant operators to get another measurement of tipped earnings for waiters and waitresses. The attached file contains the results of the nationwide survey that was fielded in 2011. Previous iterations of this survey have yielded similar results, so the Association is confident that this is a more accurate portrayal of the earnings of waiters and waitresses.

On behalf of the National Restaurant Association, I thank you for the opportunity to address your concerns, particularly on the shortcomings with current OES data. The Association is confident that, once the issues with the OES survey are resolved, the reported wage figures for waiters and waitresses will more accurately reflect their actual earnings. In the meantime, to expedite a response, please send any additional questions or concerns on the data directly to the Association, specifically to Angelo Amador, Vice President of Labor & Workforce Policy, at aamador@ restaurant.org.

Regards,

MEL SICKLER.

2011 TIPPED WAGE SURVEY

Summary of Results

Median Earnings of Waiters and Waitresses

- On a national level, the median hourly earnings of waiters and waitresses range from $16 for entry-level servers to $22 for more experienced servers.
  - Median hourly tips received by waiters and waitresses range from $12 for entry-level servers to $17 for more experienced servers.
  - The median hourly employer-paid wage ranges from $4 for entry-level servers to $5 for more experienced servers.

Median Hourly Earnings of Waiters and Waitresses
United States

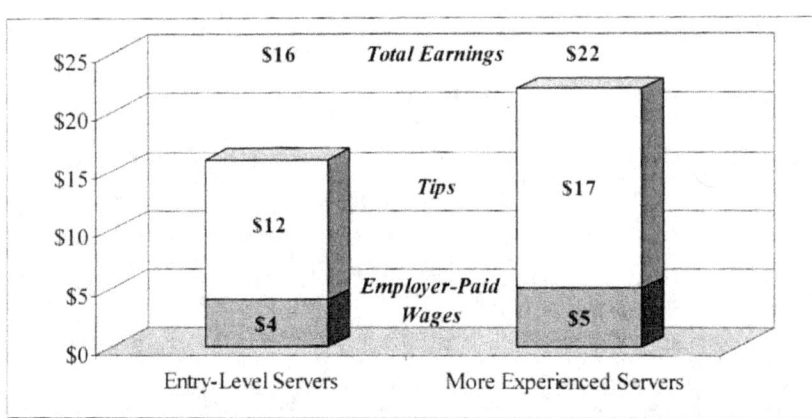

Source: National Restaurant Association, December 2011 Survey

- While these figures represent the overall averages, the hourly earnings of servers vary significantly based on the type of full-service establishment and the average per-person check size. In addition, the employer-paid wages will be higher than the national average in States that do not allow the tip credit.
- The figures are based on a nationwide survey of 409 full-service restaurants that employ waiters and waitresses who earn tips.

Research Design

This summary presents the findings of a telephone survey conducted among a national sample of 409 full-service restaurant owner/operators in the United States. The interviewing was conducted during December 2011 by Survey Sampling International, a survey research firm located in Orem, UT.

RESPONSE TO QUESTIONS OF SENATOR HARKIN BY DAVID RUTIGLIANO

Question 1. Do you think that small, predictable raises in the minimum wage that happen once a year are easier to plan for than irregular increases every 5 to 10 years?

Answer 1. Building in an increase every year only adds to the increased costs to a business, regardless of economic conditions, business level or commodity prices.

Question 2. Connecticut law requires that tipped workers receive at least 69 percent of the regular minimum wage. My bill would require 70 percent. Clearly your business has thrived under such a policy. Why do you then advocate for lower wages for others, and against a policy that would apply equally to all businesses in all States?

Answer 2. We may see a benefit if other States business cost increases. Although I am a Connecticut native I shudder to think of the consequences should our Nation follow in our economic footsteps of my home State. Connecticut is the poster child for bad economic decisions. We rank last in every category of economic growth; we have a major net migration of our young people.

Question 3. When the minimum wage goes up, does it also affect your competitors? Does a minimum wage increase put you at a competitive disadvantage?

Answer 3. We in Connecticut are undercapitalized compared to our neighboring States, this puts us at a competitive disadvantage in regards to regional expansion and growth.

[Whereupon, at 10:47 a.m., the hearing was adjourned.]